WORLD CHAMPION TACTICS

ABOUT THE AUTHORS

LEONID SHAMKOVICH

Grandmaster Leonid Shamkovich was born in Russia in 1923 and has lived in the United States since 1976. Grandmaster Leonid Shamkovich, former US Open Champion and two-time Russian Champion, is one of the most respected authorities on chess sacrifices and tactics. He quickly became a powerful force in American chess winning the US Open and many major tournaments. Shamkovich has written on the subject of chess tactics and opening theory for over 40 years, and his work has appeared in every major chess journal. He has also served as an assistant or trainer for many of the very best chessplayers.

ERIC SCHILLER

Eric Schiller, widely considered one of the world's foremost chess analysts, writers and teachers, is the author of more than 85 chess books including 15 Cardoza best-sellers. His major works include the prestigious *Batsford Chess Openings* with World Champion Garry Kasparov and Grandmaster Raymond Keene, and Cardoza Publishing's definitive series on openings, *World Champion Openings*, *Standard Chess Openings*, and *Unorthodox Chess Openings* — an exhaustive and complete opening library of more than 1700 pages! (For updated listings of all chess titles published by Cardoza Publishing, go online to www.cardozapub.com.)

OTHER CARDOZA PUBLISHING 'WORLD CHAMPION' BOOKS

WORLD CHAMPION OPENINGS *Schiller* - Covers the essential opening theory and moves of every major chess opening and variation as played by all the world champions and how you can apply them to your own games. 102 fully annotated games! 384 pages, $18.95

WORLD CHAMPION COMBINATIONS *Schiller and Keene* - Learn the insights, concepts and moves of the greatest combinations by the greatest players of all time. Complete explanations and thinking behind every combination. 84 annotated games! 264 pages, $16.95.

WORLD CHAMPION CHESS MATCHES *Gufeld* - The exciting highlights and great games of every Championship match are recounted in Gufeld's lively style, with wild anecdotes, and in-depth analysis. From a GM who has the scalps of three champions! 304 pages, $18.95.

WORLD CHAMPION TACTICS *Schiller and Shamkovich* - Packed with fascinating strategems, annotated games, and more than 500 diagrams, players learn the thinking behind the tactics of the champions and the insights to use them in their own games. 304 pages, $18.95.

WORLD CHAMPION TACTICS

Leonid Shamkovich
&
Eric Schiller

Cardoza Publishing

www.ccgames.com
play chess online with friends around the world!

Library of Congress Catalogue Card No: 98-71034
ISBN: 1-58042-005-2

TABLE OF CONTENTS

1. INTRODUCTION

Tactics are the foundation of successful chess. They are the fundamental building blocks of chess strategy, and must be mastered by all aspiring chessplayers. The thirteen official World Champions, plus Paul Morphy, the 19th century American wizard who is considered an "unofficial" World Champion, will be your guides as you learn the fundamentals of chess tactics. The journey is an important one, because a single tactical misstep can easily cost you a game, in casual or tournament competition.

This book is intended for beginning and intermediate chessplayers. Grandmaster Leonid Shamkovich, one of the world's greatest tacticians and analysts, has selected the most instructive positions and games by the World Champions. He teams up with National Master Eric Schiller, trainer of many of America's top young talent and author of dozens of books on chess, to provide a complete course in basic chess tactics.

Most books on tactics concentrate on tactical situations which are part of combinations. Combinations are complicated, and often the basic power of the individual tactic is lost in the complex beauty of a combinational setting. They are the subject of a more advanced book, *World Champion Combinations*, by Grandmaster Raymond Keene and co-author Schiller. In this book, the student will concentrate on the individual tactics, though they will sometimes be presented in the context of a complete game.

Although combinations are things of great beauty, the interaction of different tactical ideas tends to take the focus off the tactics themselves. Overwhelmed by the sacrificial brilliancy, it is easy to lose sight of the fundamental tactics which are brought together to spectacular effect. Tactics are not just used in combinations. They are used to achieve positional and strategic goals, too. This aspect of tactics is rarely discussed in books aimed at the beginner or intermediate player. It is taken for granted, when it shouldn't be.

The inherent power of a tactic, or a threatened tactic, often goes unappreciated when presented solely in the context of a brilliant game. Tactics can be found at almost any turn, and are constantly in the minds of advanced chessplayers. This book will lead you step-by-step through all of the essential tactical concepts.

We start, logically enough, with the definition of chess tactics. What are they and why do you need to use them? Then we introduce each of the essential chess tactics, showing the power of each one as used by the World Champions themselves. Each section clearly explains the important concepts of the tactic.

The second part of the book examines complete games and selected positions from the games of the World Champions. These are spectacular battles, with tactical blows all over the board. This gives the student an opportunity to see tactics at work in their natural environment.

At the end of the book you will find a set of quiz positions, followed by the solutions to the problems. You can practice your tactics by working out the complete solutions to each position, then compare your answers to the correct solutions.

2. OVERVIEW

A chess tactic is a maneuver which is designed to achieve a specific goal. It does not necessarily involve attacking an enemy piece. A **tactic** creates one or more threats that did not exist before the tactical move is made.

The crucial tactics explored in this book are shown below:

TACTICS COVERED

Fork
Pin
Discovered Check
Discovered Attack
Deflection
Decoy
Interference
X-Ray
Clearance
Blocking
Intermezzo
Desperado
Trapping a Piece
Overloading
Pursuit
Removing the Defender
Promotion
Rook Lift

3. TYPES OF TACTICS

Before we get into a discussion of each of the tactics, a few terms need to be defined, so that the discussion will be clear. Precise definitions have been offered by several authors, but they rarely agree with each other and sometimes the meaning of one author's words changes when we think in terms of another author's definitions. While we are not lobbying for our own definitions, which we formulated specifically for this book, we do want you to understand what we mean when we use some technical terms.

When you **attack** a piece you threaten to capture it. A **threat** is made when, on the next turn, a player can make a move which results in a position which is significantly better than the present situation. This may involve the capture of enemy forces, control of important squares, or damage to enemy pawn structure.

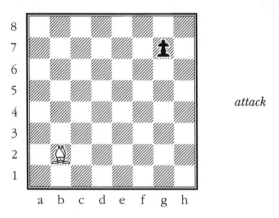

attack

A **double attack** takes place when two enemy pieces are threatened with capture on the same move. Many tactics are based on this concept. If a combination is made up of a series of tactics, then the double attack can be said to be a feature that many tactics have in common. In the diagram following, the White bishop attacks the Black queen and the Black rook.

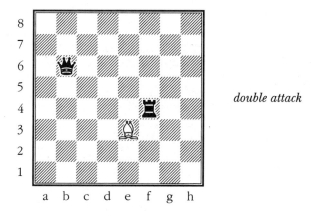

double attack

The term **double threat** is used when the attacker has two different threats as a result of the move. One of the threats is not a capture however, but something else, for example checkmate.

double threat

The White rook attacks the Black knight, and also threatens 1.Re8, checkmate.

We use the expression **mating threat** when the threat is to checkmate the enemy king in one or more moves, where there would be no way for the enemy to escape if it were still our turn. The idea is that if the opponent does not make a move which prevents the execution of the threat, the game will be won.

Consider the following position.

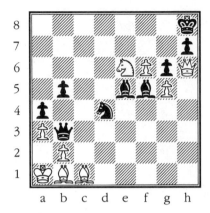

mating threat

White has two mating threats. If it is White to move, there is the pleasant choice of 1.Qg7# and 1.Qf8#. That's simple enough. Black can capture the knight at e6 with queen, bishop or knight. The first two options allow the checkmate, but taking with the knight parries both threats. Black also has a mating threat, however, and can carry it out right away!

1...Qxa3+!! Forces Black to try **2.bxa3**, since 2.Ba2 is checkmated by 2...Nb3#.

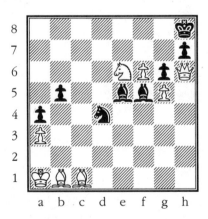

two mating threats

Black has two different mating threats! **2...Nc2+; 3.Ka2 Bxe6#** is the most poetic, removing the White knight at last, but 2...Nb3+; 3.Ka2 Nxc1# is also cute.

Many different tactics were involved in these variations, but to understand the concept of the mating threat all you need to know is that from the very first move, checkmate was inevitable.

Closely related to the mating threat is the **drawing threat.** One player threatens not to checkmate the opposing king, but to reach a technically drawn position, which might be a drawn endgame or perpetual check.

A **forced move** is a move which must be made in order to avoid immediate disaster. The international symbol for such a move is a small square (□), and many players use the term "box" to describe a forced move.

The presence of a forced move makes calculation of variations easier to carry out, because alternative strategies for the opponent can be easily dismissed. On the other hand, many moves that seem forced, especially recaptures, need not be played immediately. See the intermezzo topic later for discussion and examples of this important set of exceptions.

Now let us turn to the individual tactics and acquire the tools that will allow us to build up winning positions. From this point onward we will use games played by the World Champions to illustrate the tactics.

4. TACTICS FOR ATTACKING PIECES

DISCOVERED ATTACK

The **discovered attack** is the weaker sibling of the discovered check, which we'll meet next. In a discovered attack, the piece that finds itself under attack is not the mighty king, but a less valuable piece. That doesn't mean it can't be valuable! On the contrary, discovered attacks are much more common than discovered checks. They can also bring the enemy to their knees, as you can see below.

MAX EUWE VS. THOMAS
Hastings, 1934

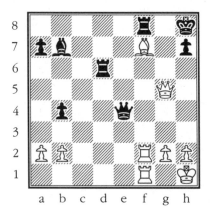

Euwe uses a discovered attack to force a quick win. He retreats the bishop from f7 to d5, uncovering an attack on the rook at f8 by the rook at f2. At the same time, the queen at e4 is attacked. Black must capture one of the attackers, but can't ward off both.

26.Bd5! Bxd5. Or 26...Rxf2; 27.Qg8#. **27.Rxf8+ Bg8; 28.Rxg8#.**

DISCOVERED CHECK

All tactics can be powerful, but a **discovered check** is usually the most powerful of all! This monster can demolish the enemy position quickly. The poor victim's resignation or checkmate is almost inevitable.

A discovered check takes place when a piece is moved, causing the enemy king to be attacked by another piece which previously had an obstructed view.

A discovered attack can involve a check, but that doesn't make it a discovered check. A discovered check only takes place if the piece which is not moved gives check as a result of another piece getting out of the way.

GERASIMOV VS VASILY SMYSLOV
Moscow, 1935

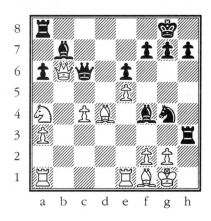

The future World Champion demonstrated the power of the discovered check with **21...Bh2+!; 22.Kh1 Be5+** and **White resigned**, because after 23.Kg1 the bishop returns to h2 with check, retreats to c7 with another discovered check and grabs the enemy queen. This repeated use of discovered checks is the theme behind the windmill combination we'll cover later on.

Sometimes a player can be tortured by repeated discovered checks, in a tactic known as a windmill. This horrible fate leaves the victim squirming helplessly as pieces fall off the board.

Windmill

The **windmill** involves repeated use of a discovered check to win material. The piece that is moved, giving discovered check, captures a piece. It then returns to the scene of the crime, also with check, before engaging in a feeding frenzy. The windmill is at the heart of many famous combinations.

C. TORRE VS. EMANUEL LASKER
Moscow, 1925

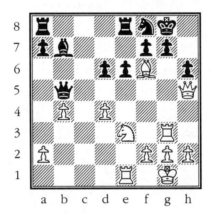

The last move, 25.Bf6!! offered up the queen. After **25...Qxh5; 26.Rxg7+** the windmill goes into motion. **26...Kh8; 27.Rxf7+ Kg8; 28.Rg7+ Kh8; 29.Rxb7+ Kg8; 30.Rg7+ Kh8.**

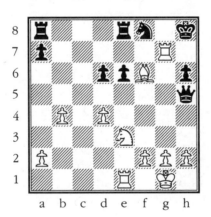

The rook could also grab the a-pawn, but that would only open a line for the Black rook on the a-file. Instead, it is time to switch directions and pick off the queen. **31.Rg5+ Kh7; 32.Rxh5 Kg6; 33.Rh3 Kxf6; 34.Rxh6+ Kg5; 35.Rh3.**

The carnage is complete and White had an easy win in the endgame, thanks to the extra pawns.

SMOTHERED MATE

The **smothered mate** is carried out by surrounding the enemy king with his own pieces, and delivering checkmate with a knight.

PAUL MORPHY VS. AN AMATEUR
Paris, 1859

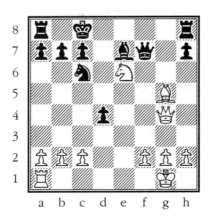

Starting with a discovered check, White arranges the entombment of the Black king, who is buried alive.

20.Nc5+! Kb8; 21.Nd7+ Kc8; 22.Nb6+! A discovered double check, which also attacks the rook at a8. But the rook must not be captured, for it is part of the plan leading to smothered mate. **22...Kb8; 23.Qc8+!!**

FORK

A **fork** is a move which attacks two pieces at once. Since the opponent can move only one piece at each turn, one of the two attacked pieces must be left to its fate. Sometimes you read that forks are a property just of knights and pawns, and another term is used when the attacker is a bishop, rook, queen or king. That is a rather artificial and useless distinction. Even if you want to distinguish short range and long range operations, the king would have to be included with the pawn and knight.

The Knight Fork

The **knight fork** is especially frequent at c7, where it gives check to the king and attacks a rook at a8.

MIKHAIL TAL VS. TIGRAN PETROSIAN
Candidates Tournament, Yugoslavia 1959

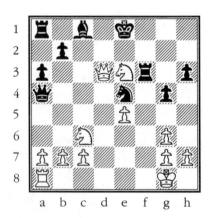

White has all sorts of available tactics here. Tal found the cleanest kill, attacking the enemy queen and forcing an exchange that led to a classic king and rook fork.

17.Qc7 Qxc7; 18.Nxc7+ Kd8; 19.Nxa8 and **White won.**

When a queen and king are both involved, then we have an example of a **royal fork.**

GARRY KASPAROV VS. TIMMAN
VSB Tournament, Amsterdam, 1994

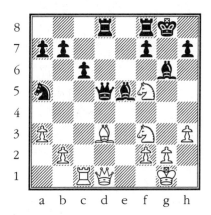

25.Ne7+ Kg7; 26.Nxd5. White had won enough material to secure victory, and the game didn't last long.

The Family Fork

One of the juiciest forks is the **family fork**, which targets a queen, king and rook.

VASILY SMYSLOV VS. KAMYSHOV
Moscow City Championship, 1945

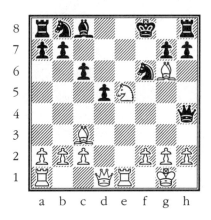

Black did not dare capture the bishop, as that would have allowed 16.Nxg6+ with a family fork.

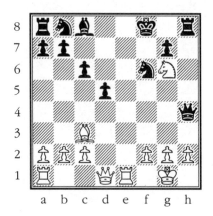

Another very common fork is at f6 (for Black) or f3 (for White), when the enemy has castled on the kingside.

Here are two examples.

GARRY KASPAROV VS. TIMMAN
Match, Prague, 1998

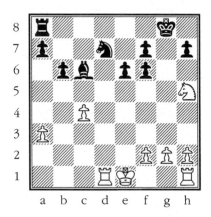

White wins material using a fork. **21.Rxd7! Bxd7; 22.Nxf6+ Kg7; 23.Nxd7.**

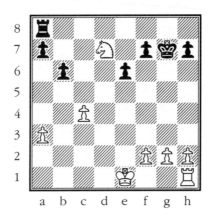

White is a piece ahead, and Black soon resigned.

ALONY VS. MIKHAIL BOTVINNIK
Tel Aviv Olympiad, 1964

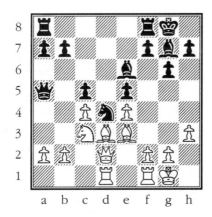

Because the White king at g1 and queen at d2 can each be attacked by a Black knight at f3, Black was able to steal a pawn with **15...Bxh3!**

The bishop cannot be captured because of 16...Nf3+, and White had no time to get rid of the knight with 16.Bxd4 because of 16...exd4; 17.gxh3 dxc3; 18.bxc3 Bxc3 and Black still has an extra pawn. Alony tried **16.b4,** which led to an interesting battle but in the end Botvinnik prevailed.

The Bishop Fork
The ability of the bishop to operate at long range makes it possible to fork two pieces on distant areas of the board.

ALEXANDER ALEKHINE VS. GADJOS
Düsseldorf, 1908

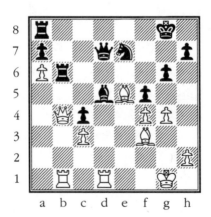

Alekhine moved his bishop into forking position with a preliminary queen sacrifice. **32.Qxe7 Qxe7; 33.Bxd5+.**

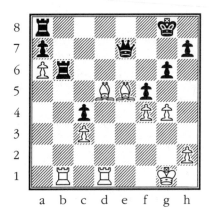

The simultaneous attack at g8 and a8 (and the pawn at c4, though that isn't relevant) wins White more material. After **33...Kf8; 34.Bxa8,** White had a rook and two bishops for the queen, and won without difficulty.

34...Qh4; 35.Bg2 Rxb1; 36.Rxb1 Qxg4; 37.h3 Qg3; 38.Bd4 Qxf4; 39.Bxa7 Qd6; 40.Ra1. Black resigned.

The Rook Fork

The rook can create a double attack in two ways. It can attack two pieces on the same straight line, or can attack one piece on a rank and another on a file. When it is really lucky, it can attack three, or even in very rare cases, four pieces at once!

EMANUEL LASKER VS. SHOWALTER
Match, New York, 1892/93

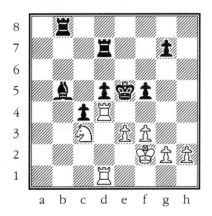

Lasker used a super rook fork with the help of a later knight fork to bring his opponent down. **37.Rxd5+!** This attacks king, rook and bishop, none of which are adequately protected.

37...Ke6. 37...Rxd5; 38.Rxd5+ Ke6; 39.Rxb5 was out of the question. **38.Nxb5! Rxd5; 39.Nc7+.** Knight fork! **39...Kd6; 40.Nxd5** Black resigned.

The Queen Fork

With the ability to work on ranks, files, and diagonals, the queen has many opportunities to create forks. In the tricky queen vs. rook endgame, the win often comes by way of a fork. In the opening, a fork at e4 or e5 can snare one of the rooks in the corner.

BORIS SPASSKY VS. KINZEL
Varna Olympiad, 1962

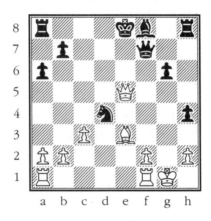

21.Qxe5+ picked off the rook at h8 and the game ended a few moves later.

The King Fork

The king operates only at close range. He sort of waddles around and hits things with his elbows. Enemy pieces can only be knocked down when there is a real crowd around the attacking king. The king forks are usually seen in the endgame, when it safe for the monarch to take an active role in the game. The king cannot attack a queen, for it would have to walk into check to do so. It can, however, attack all the other pieces, though it must approach from a safe angle.

The king fork is most common in the endgame, used against pawns.

PORTISCH VS. VASILY SMYSLOV
Hoogovens Tournament, Wijk aan Zee, 1972

White's king attacks two pawns, at b6 and c5, but the attack is not effective because the pawn at b6 is defended. Portisch quickly forced the capitulation of the former World Champion with **40.a5!**

The b-pawn cannot be defended, so **40...bxa5** was forced, but after **41.Kxc5,** Black resigned. The White king will pick off the weak Black pawns.

INTERFERENCE

The **interference** tactic places a piece on a line (rank, file or diagonal) so that it interrupts the communication of enemy pieces. Interference can be a simple tactic, as in the following position.

PORTISCH VS. BOBBY FISCHER
2nd Piatigorsky Cup, Santa Monica, 1966

The rook at e4 is defended by his colleague, but because Black has a pawn at f4, an interference is possible at e3. **28...Ne3!**

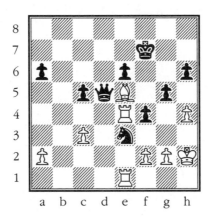

This wins material, and leads to victory after a few more moves. **29.R1xe3 fxe3; 30.Rxe3 Qxa2.** White doesn't have enough compensation, and the game didn't last long. **31.Rf3+ Ke8; 32.Bg7 Qc4; 33.hxg5 hxg5; 34.Rf8+ Kd7; 35.Ra8 Kc6.** White resigned.

PIN

A **pin** is one of the most powerful weapons in all of chess. The simple pin is at the heart of many of the most complicated combinations. A piece is *pinned* when it cannot move off of the line on which it is attacked, if the result of moving would lead to loss of a more important piece, which is a **relative** pin, or check to the king, which is an **absolute** pin. The basic method of exploiting a pin is to add as much pressure as possible to the pin.

SPRIDONOV VS. GARRY KASPAROV
European Team Championship, Skara, 1980

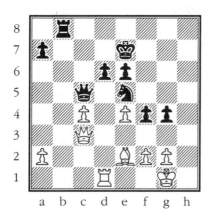

The pin at f2 (for White) or f7 (for Black) is one of the most powerful tactics. Here it leads to a crucial deflection.

35...g3!; 36...Rf1. 36.Qd4 Qxd4; 37.Rxd4 Rb2 is a winning fork that is also a skewer. 38.Kf1 loses to a double deflection. 38...f3! The bishop cannot move, so the pawn is forced to abandon g2. 39.gxf3 (39.Bxf3 Rxf2+; 40.Ke1 Rxf3!; 41.gxf3 Nxf3+ finishes with a fork.) 39.g2+! The threat of the pawn promotion deflects the king from the bishop. **36.gxf2+; 37.Rxf2.** The rook is pinned, so the back rank is exposed.

37.Rb1+; 38.Bf1. The bishop is now pinned. **38.Qe3!** The queen is deflected, and the c-pawn is lost. **39.Qxe3.** 39.Qa5 Rb2; 40.Qc7+ Nd7 runs out of checks, and the penalty is the rook at f2. **39.fxe3; 40.Rc2.**

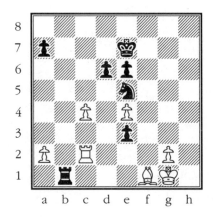

The pawn seems to be defended. **40.Nxc4!** White resigned. After 41.Rxc4 e2 Black gets a new queen.

Absolute Pin

An **absolute pin** is a pin against the king. These pins cannot be broken by moving the attacked piece. The absolute pin is a consequence of the rules. A player may not move in such a way as to leave the king in check at the conclusion of the move. Absolute pins play a major role in the opening, where they are used to tie down enemy pieces and prevent them from advancing.

BUDZINSKY VS. PAUL MORPHY
Paris, 1859
King's Gambit Declined
1.e4 e5; 2.f4 exf4; 3.Bc4 d5; 4.Bxd5 Nf6; 5.Nc3 Bb4; 6.d3.

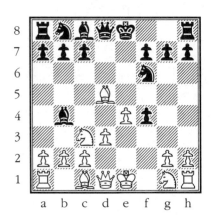

This creates an absolute pin at c3. Because the knight cannot move, the bishop at d5 and pawn at e4 have less support.

6...Nxd5; 7.exd5 0–0; 8.Qf3 Re8+; 9.Nge2.

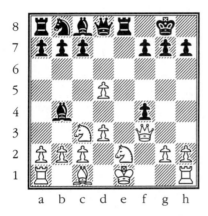

A second absolute pin is added, this time along the e-file. Remember that the knight is not really protected by its colleague at c3, because that piece is also pinned by the bishop at b4.

9...Bxc3+; 10.bxc3 Qh4+; 11.g3. Black ignores the threat to the queen and continues the attack. **11...Bg4.**

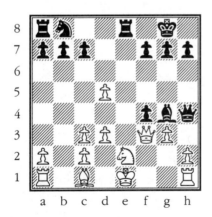

Black exploits the pin on e2 by adding one at f3. If the queen moves, then Black wins material by capturing first at g3, then at e2. White actually resigned here, but let's consider what might have happened. **12.Qf2.** (12.gxh4 Bxf3 wins either the rook at h1 or the knight at e2.) **12...fxg3; 13.Qg2; 13.hxg3 Qxh1+** shows yet another pin being exploited — this time on the h-file. 13...Rxe2+; 14.Qxe2 Bxe2; 15.Kxe2 g2; 16.Rg1 Qxh2; 17.Be3 Nd7 with a queen and two pawns for a mere rook.

Relative Pin

The **relative pin** involves a pin against a piece other than the king. The pinned piece can move, but only at the cost of exposing a piece of greater value to attack. The most common relative pin involves a White bishop at g5, Black knight at f6, and Black queen at d8. The power of this pin is seen in many openings, including one named after Botvinnik himself, the Botvinnik Variation of the Semi-Slav Defense.

DENKER VS. MIKHAIL BOTVINNIK
United States vs. Soviet Union, Radio Match, 1945
Semi-Slav Defense: Botvinnik Variation
1.d4 d5; 2.c4 e6; 3.Nc3 c6; 4.Nf3 Nf6; 5.Bg5.

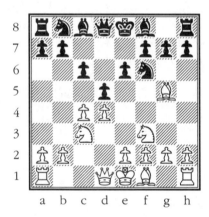

The Botvinnik Variation is crucially concerned with this pin and its consequences. It leads to wild complications early in the game, all because of the pressure on the kingside.

5...dxc4. Black boldly accepts the pawn. **6.e4.** White threatens to exploit the pin by advancing the e-pawn to e5. **6...b5.** Black ignores the threat, hanging on to the pawn.

7.e5 h6!

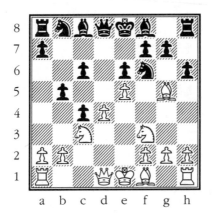

This key move pushes back the bishop, breaking the pin.

8.Bh4 g5; 9.Nxg5! White sacrifices a knight to re-establish the pin. **9...hxg5; 10.Bxg5.**

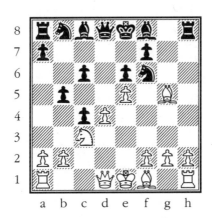

White has renewed the pin and will win the knight.

10...Nbd7; 11.exf6 Bb7. The stage is now set for a complicated middlegame. Let's see how Botvinnik continued the game, using a flurry of tactics.

12.Be2 Qb6; 13.0-0 0-0-0; 14.a4 b4!; 15.Ne4 c5; 16.Qb1!

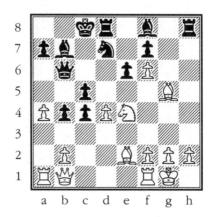

White removes his queen from the dangerous d-file, where the Black rook is stationed, and also protects his Knight at e4.

16...Qc7. Black is wasting no time, and aiming for direct attack, already threatening mate at h2. **17.Ng3.** White defends against the mate by retreating the knight, which is now pinned to h2.

17...cxd4; 18.Bxc4. The bishop cannot be captured because of the absolute pin Rc1. Instead, Botvinnik adjusts his sights, with a new target at g2. **18...Qc6.** White replied **19.f3** and for the rest you'll have to wait for the quiz section. White did not last long!

Terminal Pin

There is one pin which doesn't clearly fit either the class of absolute pin or the class of relative pin. This is a pin not against a king, but against a mating square. It might be called a **terminal pin**, because moving the pinned piece will terminate the game. We saw an example of it in the previous game, after move 17 by White.

DENKER VS. MIKHAIL BOTVINNIK
United States vs. Soviet Union, Radio Match, 1945

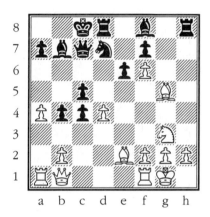

There is a terminal pin against the knight at g3, because of the threatened mate at h2.

St. Andrew's Cross

The **St. Andrew's cross** involves two pins, one against the enemy king and another against a second piece. It has been seen in a number of games, and is hard to anticipate.

JOSE CAPABLANCA VS. ALEXANDER ALEKHINE
World Championship, 1927

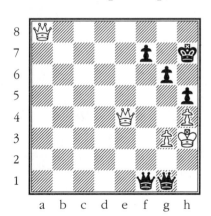

Capablanca, as White, resigned, because if he blocked the check with 67.Qg2, then 67...Qa1 is checkmate.

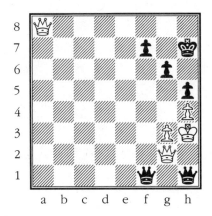

The king pin is on the f1-h3 diagonal, while the pin against the queen at a8 is on the h1-a8 diagonal.

Oblique Cross

The **oblique cross** also involves a diagonal pin, but has a rank or file pin as its partner.

ALAPIN VS. ALEXANDER ALEKHINE
St. Petersburg International, Russia, 1914

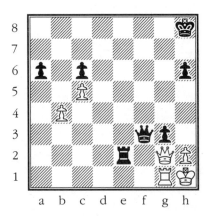

White resigned, because if the Black queen is captured, then the Black rook delivers mate at h2.

Triple Pin

ALEXANDER ALEKHINE VS. CERCLE DE MONTMORTE
Blindfold Simultaneous Exhibition, Paris, France, 1925

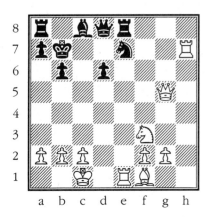

The knight is pinned three times. The rook at e1 applies a pin on the e-file. Its compatriot at h7 uses the seventh rank. The queen applies the pressure along the h4-d8 diagonal.

REMOVING THE DEFENDER
The tactic of **removing the defender** is a simple and logical concept. If a piece is defended, the elimination of the guardian can lead to the win of material. This tactic is very common in all stages of the game, and is often part of the battle for the initiative in the opening. Consider the standard Spanish Game.

1.e4 e5; 2.Nf3 Nc6; 3.Bb5.

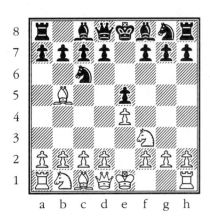

The idea of removing the defender is at the heart of this opening strategy. White threatens to capture the knight and then the pawn at e5. Although this fails for tactical reasons at the moment, since 4.Bxc6 dxc6; 5.Nxe5 can be met by 5...Qd4, the threat awakens after **3...a6; 4.Ba4 Nf6; 5.0-0,** which is the normal continuation.

TRAPPED PIECES

When a piece has no escape route, it is **trapped**. If a king is trapped and in check, the result is checkmate. When the trapped piece is something other than the king, the piece may be captured. It may also be left to rot, having no significant role in the game.

Trapped Knight

The knight is easy to trap at the edge of the board because it has very few moves. In the corner, there are only two possible escape squares, and they are easily covered. The king can trap a knight all by himself.

PAUL MORPHY VS BOTTIN
Paris, 1858

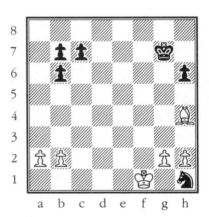

Black's knight is trapped and White wins. The game lasted just a few more moves before Black acknowledged defeat. **27.g4 Kg6; 28.Kg2 h5; 29.h3.** Black resigned.

Trapped Bishop

The bishop has a greater range than the knight, but can still be trapped in squares near the corner. To trap a bishop, you must take away all but one of the available diagonals. On the edge of the board, there are never more than two available diagonals, so you just need to close one of them. In the corner of the board, the bishop has only a single diagonal.

CORZO VS. JOSE CAPABLANCA
Havana, 1902

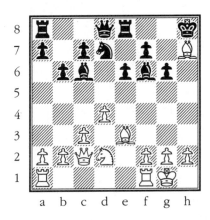

White had just played Bxh7, and Black responded by advancing the g-pawn to g6. The bishop is trapped at h7, and cannot escape.

In such cases White usually sacrifices it for the remaining kingside pawns, but this did not achieve enough compensation in the present game.

Trapped Rook

The rook is a little harder to trap than the bishop. It is possible, however, to use a minor piece to close the lines, since then a sacrifice of the exchange can be forced.

GARRY KASPAROV VS. KORCHNOI
World Championship Semifinal, London, 1983

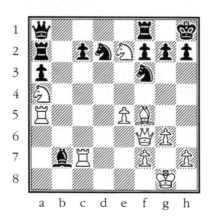

The rook at a7 is trapped, and if the queen moves to allow the rook to retreat, the bishop at b2 falls.

22...Qe8. Of course not 22...Qb8??; 23.Nec6! **23.Rxb2 Qxe7; 24.Nc6.** The fork wins the exchange. **24...Qc5; 25.Nxa7 Qxa7; 26.e5** and the game didn't last long.

26...Ng8; 27.Be3 Qa8; 28.Qxa8 Rxa8; 29.f4 Ne7; 30.Rd2 and Black resigned.

Trapped Queen

Trapping the ultra-mobile queen is no easy task. She can slip and slide and do everything except jump over pieces, which would be an unsuitable motion for a lady.

RENMAN VS. GARRY KASPAROV
European Team Championship, Skara, 1980

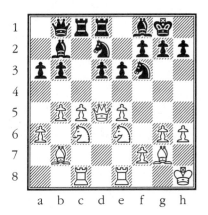

White's pawn at c5 should prevent Black from using that square for the knight, threatening a fork at b3. Unfortunately, the position of the White queen lets Kasparov play it anyway.

23...Nc5!; 24.Rc2. 24. bxc5 dxc5 leaves the queen with no retreat. **24...e5.** The queen must retreat and the e-pawn falls. **25.Qd1.**

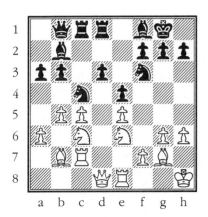

25...Ncxe4; 26.Nxe4 Bxe4; 27.Bxe4 Nxe4 and Kasparov went on to win.

Trapped King

When a king is trapped, then all that is needed is a check to finish it off. That's checkmate! The most famous trapped king example is the **smothered mate**. The king, surrounded by friendly forces, is suffocated by an enemy knight.

Here is an example from Morphy:

PAUL MORPHY VS. AMATEUR
Casual Game, Paris March 1859

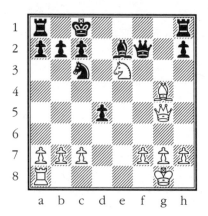

Starting with a discovered check, White arranges the entombment of the Black king, who is buried alive.

20.Nc5+! Kb8; 21.Nd7+ Kc8; 22.Nb6+! A discovered double check, which also attacks the rook at a8. But the rook must not be captured, for it is part of the plan leading to smothered mate.

22...Kb8; 23.Qc8+!!

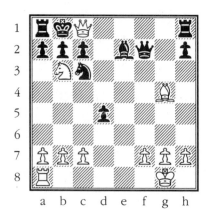

This is the key position of a smothered mate. Black must capture the queen with the rook, because she is protected by the knight at b6. **23...Rxc8; 24.Nd7#.**

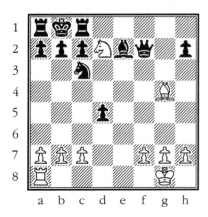

Smothered mate is one of the most embarrassing mates. No one likes to get caught in this compromising position!

X-RAY ATTACK

The **x-ray** attack, also known as a **skewer**, turns a line of enemy pieces into shish kabob. One piece sees right through an enemy piece, exerting control over a more distant square, where the unsuspecting enemy piece gets snared. Since only the knight can jump over a friendly piece, you'd think this would be a knight tactic, but it isn't. In fact, the knight, along with the king and pawn, are not able to execute an x-ray. Queens, rooks and bishops are the only ones allowed to participate in this tactic.

BOBBY FISCHER VS. BISGUIER
United States Championship, 1963/64

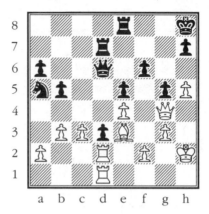

The focus of the x-ray is at d7. **34.Rxd3 Qxd3; 35.Qxd7.**

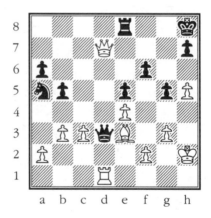

Black resigned. Although White only has an extra pawn, Black is forced to exchange queens. 35...Qxd7; 36.Rxd7. The endgame is a simple win. The rook can go after weak pawns, the king can get to f5, and the bishop can get to b6 and set up further exchanges.

5. TACTICS FOR ATTACKING THE KING

DESTROYING THE BARRIER

The destruction of an enemy pawn barrier is a strategic goal which is often accomplished by a special tactic designed for the demolition of the pawn structure. The tactic usually consists of more than one move, because a barrier has more than one pawn. Usually two or more defenders must be swept aside in order to get at the enemy king.

BIRD VS. PAUL MORPHY
London, 1858

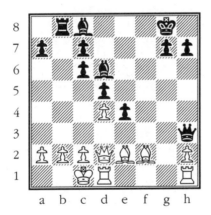

Black has two only two pawns for the rook, but the queenside is filled with attacking possibilities. Morphy offers the queen to destroy the barrier.

18...Qa3!!; 19.c3. 19.bxa3?? would of course lead to mate by 19...Bxa3#. **19...Qxa2; 20.b4!** Bird defends persistently, offering an exchange of queens. Morphy has placed his hope in a long-term attack and does not mind the material deficit. **20...Qa1+; 21.Kc2 Qa4+.**

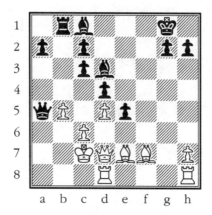

The White king cannot escape from the queenside jail.

22.Kb2? Forced was 22.Kc1, trying to get a draw by perpetual check. Black would continue with 22...a5! with a powerful attack, a sample line going 23.Qc2 Qa3+; 24.Qb2 (A pretty line is 24.Kd2 axb4; 25.Ra1 bxc3+; 26.Ke3 Bf4+!; 27.Kxf4 Qd6+; 28.Ke3 Qh6#)

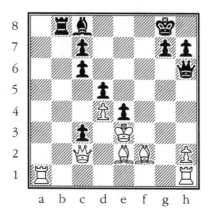

24...axb4!; 25.Qxa3. (25.cxb4 Qa4! keeps the queens on the board, and after the fall of the pawn at b4 the king will be stripped of his defenders and eventually checkmated.) 25...bxa3. Black, with four pawns for the rook, continues to have unpleasant threats based on a combination of ...Rb2, ...Rb3, ...Bf4+, and...a2. 26.Be3 Rb3; 27.Kd2 Rb2+; 28.Ke1 a2; 29.Ra1.

The rook at h1 is overworked because it must remain on the first rank to meet Black's ...Rb1+ can be countered by Kf2. This allows Black to play 29...Bxh2. Five pawns for the rook, and plenty of threats remain! 30.Kd1 c5; 31.Bc1! (31.dxc5 Bd7 and the bishop will come to a4, so White must try 32.Rxa2 Rxa2; 33.Rxh2 but 33...Bb5 is a difficult endgame for White.) 31...Rb1; 32.Rxa2 Bf4; 33.Kc2 and Black is forced to play 33...Rxc1+; 34.Rxc1 Bxc1; 35.Kxc1 with a lost game.

22...Bxb4!

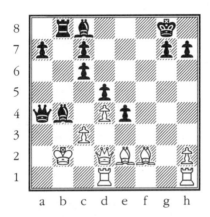

Black demolishes the pawn barrier to open up lines for the heavy pieces. **23.cxb4 Rxb4+; 24.Qxb4.** White has no choice. 24.Kc1 Qa1+; 25.Kc2 Qb2#. **24...Qxb4+; 25.Kc2.** White has two rooks and a bishop for the queen and seven pawns, but material is a secondary consideration as the attack continues.

25...e3! A clearance opens up the b1–h7 diagonal. **26.Bxe3 Bf5+; 27.Rd3.** White loses a bishop after 27.Bd3 Qc4+; 28.Kb2 Bxd3 and it only gets worse: 29.Rd2 Qb4+; 30.Kc1 Qb1#. **27...Qc4+; 28.Kd2 Qa2+!** The king is forced back to the first rank, as otherwise the bishop at e2 falls, and its companion is also doomed.

29.Kd1. Now White will have to part with his rook on h1. **29...Qb1+.** White resigned. Black will just take the rook and the h2-pawn after which he has a commanding lead in material.

DOUBLE CHECK

A **double check** involves two pieces simultaneously attacking the enemy king. This type of check can never be headed by a queen or rook, as in that case the enemy king would already be in check.

Nor can it involve a pawn, unless the pawn is involved in a capture. So the most common double checks are delivered by minor pieces. A double check is always a discovered check, which makes sense because a player can only move one piece on a turn, and the enemy king cannot be in check when it is the player's turn to move.

EMANUEL LASKER VS. MARSHALL
St. Petersburg International, Russia, 1914

Marshall had resigned a move earlier, but had he continued he would not have been able to avoid this position. White promotes the pawn to a queen and executes a double check and mate.

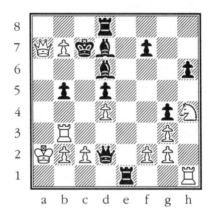

PURSUIT

Pursuit is a tactic used to save a lost game. It involves attacking an enemy piece relentlessly. While the piece cannot be captured, the enemy must move it at each turn, and therefore can do nothing to try to win the game. If a piece can escape the pursuit, the tactic fails. The most common form of pursuit is perpetual check.

PERPETUAL CHECK

In a **perpetual check**, the king cannot avoid a check no matter where it moves. The game ends in a draw, because inevitably a three-fold repetition or 50-move rule draw will arise.

PORTISCH VS. GARRY KASPAROV
Alekhine Memorial, Moscow, 1971

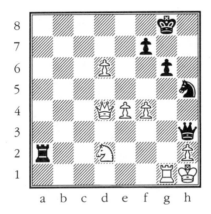

Black forces a draw by perpetual check.

42...Rxd2; 43.Qxd2. White must capture, as otherwise there is mate at h2. **43...Qf3+; 44.Qg2.** 44.Rg2 Qf1+; 45.Rg1 Qf3+ will lead to a quick repetition, otherwise **44...Ng3+!** The knight is sacrificed, but all Black needs is the queen. **45.hxg3.**

45...Qh5+; 46.Qh2 Qf3+; 47.Rg2 Qd1+; 48.Qg1 Qh5+; 49.Rh2 Qf3+. Draw agreed. White just can't stop the checks.

HARASSMENT

When the target is a piece other than the king, we can use the term **harassment**. In this case a piece of greater value than the attacker is threatened move after move. While perpetual check is not uncommon, examples of harassment are extremely rare in the games of the World Champions.

6. TACTICS FOR CONTROLLING SQUARES

BLOCKING

The **block** is a device which places a piece on a square so that an enemy pawn stationed in front of it cannot advance. This takes advantage of the unique character of pawn captures. Since a pawn cannot capture a piece standing right in front of it, and cannot move forward onto an occupied square, it is stuck in place. This is a tactic mostly used in defense, but it is sometimes seen in spectacular combinations. The most famous example is the following.

BOBBY FISCHER VS. BENKO
United States Championship, 1963

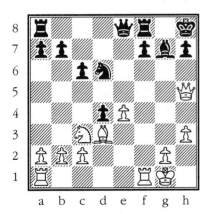

White would love to advance the pawn to e5 and deliver checkmate at h7, but Black is ready to reply with ...f5, closing the crucial diagonal. Fischer applies a block to eliminate that plan.

19. Rf6!! The rook must not be captured because then 20.e5! would win. **19...Kg8; 20.e5 h6.** 20.Bxf6 21. Qxh7#. **21.Ne2!**

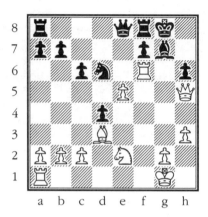

There is no defense, so Black resigned. 21...Bxf6 allows 22. Qxh6 after which mate cannot be avoided.

CHOKE

The idea behind the **choke** is that a piece will take away a flight square from the enemy king. The choke is applied so that other pieces can come in and finish the mating attack.

MAX EUWE VS. BOBBY FISCHER
New York 1957

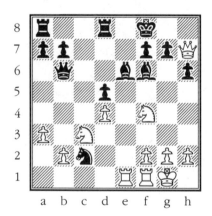

Black has just captured a bishop at c2 and anticipates White's recapture wuth the queen. Instead, young Fischer gets mated by Euwe.

19.Ncxd5. The knight at d5 chokes the e7 square, and Qh8# is available. **19...Rxd5; 20.Nxd5.** Black resigned. If the knight is captured then Qh8 is checkmate.

Our next example is a little more involved. White does not have the advantage of open files to use in the attack.

MIKHAIL TAL VS. TIMMAN
Chess Olympiad, Skopje, Yugoslavia, 1972

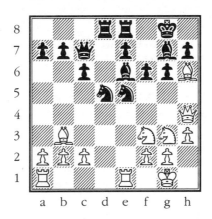

Tal needed to get the knight to g5, where it would attack the bishop at g6, and remove f7 as a flight square for the enemy king. The problem is that Black has a pawn at f6 guarding the square. The pawn also guards the knight at e5. There is no time to lose, because Timman might be able to thwart Tal's plan if allowed to play ...Nxf3+. So Tal played **18.Rxe5!!** and after **18...fxe5,** the knight reached its goal with **19.Ng5.**

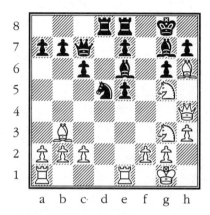

There is now the immediate threat of 20.Nxe6, and also a threat of 20.Bxg7 followed by 21.Qxh7+. This would not have a great effect if the Black king could escape via f7, but the choke prevents that.

Timman tried **19...Bf6** but after **20.Nxe6** realized that he had a hopeless position and resigned.

CLEARANCE

Many times you will find that some of your own forces are just in the way of your attack. **Clearance** is the tactic used to move them aside so that other pieces can make use of a square or line. As part of a combination, the move that clears the square is accompanied by threats, but the basic tactic of gaining access to a critical square by getting a piece out of the way can be seen in simpler forms, too.

GARRY KASPAROV VS. HJORTH
World Junior Championship, Adelaide, 1980

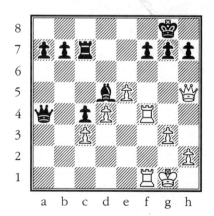

White has an extra exchange, but with only one open file it is no match for Black's queenside pawns. White opens lines with a tremendous clearance, throwing caution and pawns to the wind.

22.e6! What is surprising about this move is that it seems to contribute nothing to the task of deflecting the bishop from f7. In fact, however, it opens up the d5-square so that the White pawn can chase the bishop from the key square.

22...Bxe6; 23.d5 Qb5. 23...Rc5 creates a nice pin against the pawn, but 24.Rxf7! gives Black no time to exploit it. 23.g6 drives the queen back. 24.Qh4 with the threat of Qd8+, and the bishop is still under assault.

24...Rh4! A new threat is created at h7 while the queen is defended so that the pin on the d-pawn dissolves. **24...Qc5+.** 24.Qxd5; 25.Qxh7+ Kf8; 26.Rd4 pins the queen to d8. That square is not the destination of the rook, however! 26...Qc5 pins the rook and eliminates the possibility of Rd8+. The rook doesn't have to participate, however, just sit and watch. 27.Qh8+ Ke7; 28.Qd8#.

25.Rf2 Bxd5. This is playable, because the rook at f2 is pinned. White unpins by creating a new and deadly pin! **26.Rd4!** This breaks the pin at f2 while exploiting the pin along the 5th rank. **26.Rd7.** The only move.

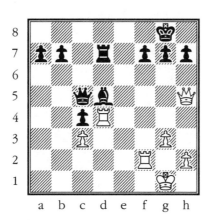

Tal played **27.Rf5** and Black resigned. The bishop is lost.

Our next example comes from the same wizard of tactical play.

MIKHAIL TAL VS. TOLUSH
Soviet Championship, 1957

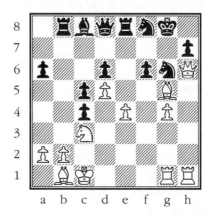

To attack, you need to use as many pieces as possible. White has queen, bishop, and a pair of rooks in attacking position. Black defends with two knights, and potentially two rooks and a queen on the seventh rank. To win, White needs the assistance of the knight and bishop on the queenside. The knight wants to go to e4, and the bishop needs the diagonal to be open. White must clear the e4 square to accomplish these goals. The fact that the bishop is hanging is simply of no significance.

30.e5! Rxe5. The other captures lose quickly. 30...fxg5; 31. Bxg6 hxg6 (31...Nxg6; 32.Qxh7+ Kf8; 33.Qxg6) 32.Qh8+ Kf7; 33.Rh7+ Nxh7; 34.Qxh7+ Kf8; 35.Rf1+ Bf5; 36.gxf5 and mate follows in six moves or less. 30...dxe5; 31.Bxg6 hxg6; 32.Qh8+ Kf7; 33.Rh7+ Nxh7; 34.Qxh7+ Kf8; 35.Bh6#. 30...fxe5 is not on because of the pin, as 31.Bxd8 snares the queen and checkmates shortly thereafter.

31.Bxg6.

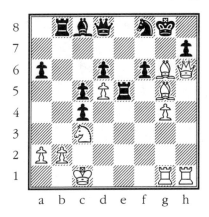

The bishop enters with devastating effect. Neither bishop can be captured. 31...hxg6; 32.Qh8+ Kf7; 33.Rh7+ Ke8 (33...Nxh7; 34.Qxd8 Nxg5; 35.Qc7+) 34.Bh6 with a winning pin. Or 31...Rxg5; 32.Bxh7+.

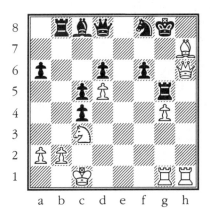

32...Nxh7; 33.Qxh7+ Kf8; 34.Ne4 Rg8; 35.Rf1 Rb7; 36.Qh6+ Rbg7; 37.Nxf6 wraps things up in a few moves.

Consider the flight of the king instead. It too must be rejected. 32...Kf7 which meets with the vigorous 33.Ne4 Rxd5; 34.Bg8+! Kxg8; 35.Nxf6+ and 36.Nxd5 with a winning position.

So Tolush chose **31...Rb7;** hoping to defend along the seventh rank. Tal replied **32.Ne4.**

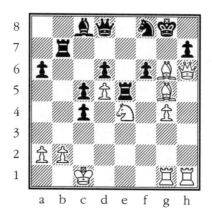

Both of the minor pieces are major players in the attack. Black has nothing better than capturing at g5.

32...fxg5. 32.Rxg5; 33.Nxg5 fxg5; 34.Bf5 is clearly better for White, but not nearly as bad as the position Black gets in the game. **33.Rf1 Rxe4.** There wasn't much choice. 33...Nxg6; 34.Nf6+ forces Black to give up the queen for the knight.

34.Bxe4 Rg7; 35.Rf6 Bxg4. Black could have pushed the c-pawn to open some lines against the White king, but it wouldn't have changed the final outcome. **36.Rhf1 Nd7; 37.Rxd6.** The weak pawns are mowed down.

37...Qe7; 38.Rxa6 Kh8; 39.Bxh7 Nb8. 39...Rxh7 loses to 40. Ra8+. **40.Bf5+.** The discovered check allows the bishop to transfer to e6. **40...Kg8; 41.Be6+ Bxe6; 42.Rxe6.** Black resigned.

Square Clearance

GARRY KASPAROV VS. MARTINOVIC
Baku, 1980

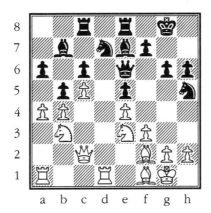

The knight at d7 is the key to the position. It is under attack from the rook at d1, and is presently protected only by the queen. A clearance is required.

25.Nc4! Rc7. 25...bxc4?; 26.Bxc4 Qf6; 27.Rxd7 is not just an extra pawn for White. 27...Rb8; 28.Na5 Bc8; 29.Rc7 Rxb4; 30.Nxc6! Rb7; 31.Nxe7+ and the knight cannot be captured, so White is a piece up.

26.Nd6. The fork at e8 and b7 is significant, because the bishop though bad, helps guard the queenside. After **26...Rb8; 27.axb5 cxb5; 28.Nxb7 Rbxb7; 29.Qa2!** it was all over but the shouting.

29...Nb8 saved the pawn but the rook at b7 runs out of room. **30.Na5! Qxa2; 31.Rxa2 Ra7.** Saving Black's queenside is beyond the power of mere mortals. 31...Rd7 is met by 32.Rd5.

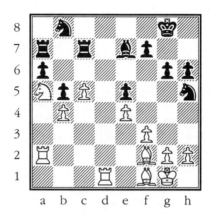

32.c6! Discovered attack on the rook. **32...Ra8; 33.Rc2!** An excellent move. Kasparov gives up the b-pawn for access to d8. Black accepts the decoy.

33...Bxb4. 33...Nf6; 34.Bc5 Bxc5+; 35.Rxc5 wins the e-pawn. **34.Rd8+ Kg7; 35.Bb6.** Black is forced into an unfavorable liquidation.

35...Bxa5; 36.Bxa5 Rxc6; 37.Rxb8 Rxb8; 38.Rxc6 b4; 39.Bc7. Black resigned, as the pawns start to fall.

Rank Clearance

The **rank clearance** is somewhat rare, but it is an effective tactic when the opportunity arises. Our example was seen earlier in the section on the oblique cross.

ALAPIN VS. ALEXANDER ALEKHINE
St. Petersburg International, Russia, 1914

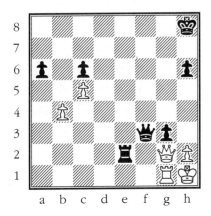

White resigned, because if the Black queen is captured, then the second rank is cleared and the Black rook delivers mate at h2.

File Clearance

ANATOLY KARPOV VS. SALOV
Linares, 1993

White would give anything to get one of the rooks to h8 and deliver mate. The investment of a queen is a small price to pay.

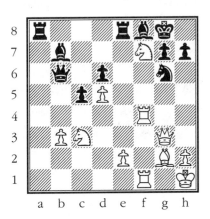

33.Qxg6!! This brilliant sacrifice ends the game. There is no defense, for example 33...hxg6; 34.Rh4 and mate next.

Diagonal Clearance

GARRY KASPAROV VS. SMIRIN
Soviet Championship, 1988

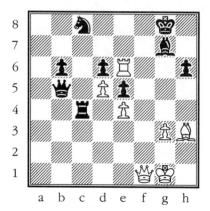

39.Rxh6!! Clearance of e6 so that Be6 can be played. **39...Bxh6; 40.Be6+ Kh8; 41.Qf6+.**

DEFLECTION

A **deflection** is exactly what the term implies. A piece is forced to leave its post, and the defensive formation falls apart.

PAUL MORPHY VS. JOUNOUD
Paris, 1858

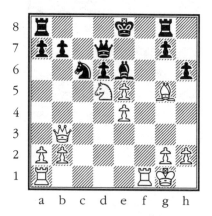

16.Nc7+! Qxc7. The king has no legal move, so the capture is forced. The deflection of the queen leaves the bishop at e6 unguarded.

17.Qxe6+. Black resigned, because of the triple attack on the king, rook and pawn at d6. The game might have concluded 17...Ne7; 18.Bxe7 Qxe7; 19.Qxg8+ Kd7; 20.Qxa8 with two extra rooks and checkmate in the near future.

The goal may be to remove a defender, or a blockader, as in the next position.

MIKHAIL BOTVINNIK VS. JOSE CAPABLANCA
AVRO Tournament, Holland, 1938

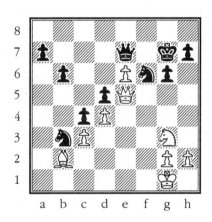

30.Ba3!! Qxa3. Or 30...Qe8; 31.Qc7+ Kg8; 32.Be7 Ng4; 33.Qd7. **31.Nh5+ gxh5.** 31...Kh6 also loses. 32.Nxf6 Qc1+; 33.Kf2 Qd2+; 34.Kg3 Qxc3+; 35.Kh4 Qxd4+; 36.Ng4+. 31...Kh8 walks into 32.Qxf6+ Kg8; 33.Qg7#.
32.Qg5+ Kf8; 33.Qxf6+ Kg8; 34.e7!

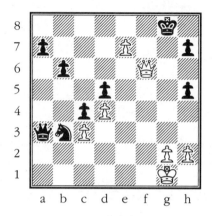

There is nothing to fear from checks!

34...Qc1+; 35.Kf2 Qc2+. Black fares no better on **35...Qd2+; 36.Kg3 Qe1+.** 36...Qxc3+; 37.Kh4 Qe1+; 38.Kxh5 and there are no more checks. 37.Kh3 Qxc3+ is met by the winning move 38.g3! **36.Kg3 Qd3+; 37.Kh4 Qe4+; 38.Kxh5 Qe2+; 39.Kh4 Qe4+; 40.g4 Qe1+; 41.Kh5.** Black resigned.

DECOY

The **decoy** is the reverse deflection. The idea here is to lure a piece into a trap, to place it on a square where it will be subject to attack as part of a tactical combination.

FISCHER VS. SHOCRON
Mar del Plata, 1959

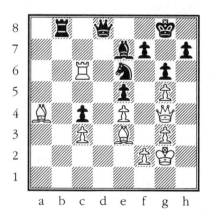

White starts with a decoy sacrifice, intended to draw the enemy pawn from f7 to e6. **39.Rxe6! Qc8.** Black replies with a pin, hoping to be able to capture at e6 with the queen. Note that Rxg6+ is not now a threat, because the queen on the eighth rank is protected by the rook.

On 39...fxe6; 40.Qxe6+ Kf8; 41.Qxe5 Kf7, White has the tremendous deflection 42.Bd7! The threat is Be6+. 42...Qxd7; 43.Qxb8 Qd3; 44.Qe5 is a winning position for White.

40.Bd7!! A brilliant decoy, bringing the queen to d7, when Rxg6+ wins the queen via a discovered attack. Black resigned.

7. MISCELLANEOUS TACTICS

DESPERADO

A piece in a desperate situation can become a **desperado**. A desperado is a move by a piece which is going to be captured anyway. Instead of standing in place awaiting the fatal blow, the piece makes an exit with a flourish and inflicts serious damage on the opponent.

GARRY KASPAROV VS. PRIBYL
European Team Championship, Skara, 1980

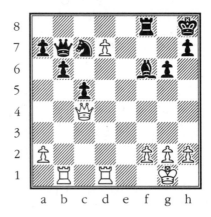

In this position White is naturally tempted to capture the c-pawn since the pawn at b6 is pinned. However, 25.Qxc5? would allow Black a powerful desperado with 25...Qxg2+! sacrificing the queen for a pawn before capturing the White queen. Kasparov avoided the trap and simply continued 25.Rd6, winning without difficulty.

INTERMEZZO

The concept of an in-between move has been one of the joys of chess since the early days. There is something especially pleasing about being able to ignore an opponent's threat to create one of your own. The chess literature has many terms for this concept, including the German "zwischenzug" (tsvi-shen-tsuug) and English "in between move", both of which are somewhat awkward. I prefer the Italian term, **intermezzo,** which is elegant and easy to pronounce. Sometimes the tactic is described as an intermediate move, which engenders confusion between the tactic and the evaluation of a move as recommended for beginners or more advanced players.

By any name, the intermezzo is one of the most exquisite and highly prized of tactics. It requires a very disciplined mind to constantly keep in mind that a capture need not be followed by an immediate recapture when one is available. The intermezzo is the tactic most frequently overlooked, even by top professionals.

GARRY KASPAROV VS. SHORT
Thessaloniki, Olympiad, 1988

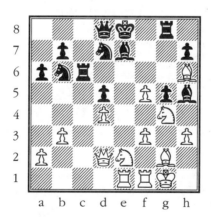

The bishop at h6 seems to be trapped and is under attack by the rook at c6.

23.Ng3! Black resigned. 23...Bxg4; 24.Bxg5! An intermezzo which sets up a pin. 24...Rxg5. 24...Bxh3; 25.Bxe7; 25.Qxg5 Kf8; 26.f6! Bxf6; 27.fxg4! The final pin wins.

An intermezzo can take place even in the opening, as the following example shows.

GELLER VS. TIGRAN PETROSIAN
Spartakiad, Moscow, 1963

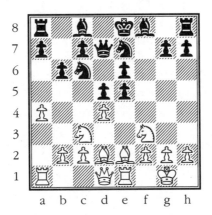

Black has just captured at e5, the culmination of a faulty plan that created a structural mess. Petrosian must have expected White to recapture, as otherwise the pawn can advance to a permanent home at e4. Geller found an amazing intermezzo.

11. Bb5!! Ng6. Black's only chance for survival. 11...e4 gets smashed on the diagonals. 12. Ne5! attacks the queen and the knight at c6 cannot do anything about it because of the pin. 12...Qd6; 13.Bf4! The threat of discovered attack against the Black queen leaves her with no useful moves. 11...exd4; 12. Nxd4 Qd6 (12...a6; 13.Bxc6 Nxc6; 14.Nxe6 would force Black to give up the queen. 14...Qxe6; 15. Rxe6+ Bxe6; 16. Qe2 Kd7; 17.Re1 Re8 seems to hang in, but the bishop at e6 is pinned so 18.Nxd5 can be played.) 13.Nxc6 Nxc6; 14.Bf4 Qd7;15.Qxd5. **12.Nxe5 Ngxe5; 13.Rxe5!**

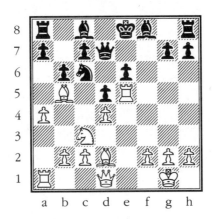

This can be safely played because of the pin at c6. Now the e-pawn is pinned, so Nxd5 becomes a threat.

13...a6. 13...Be7; 14.Qf3 Bf6 (14...Bb7; 15.Rae1); 15.Nxd5 Bxe5; 16.Nf6+. 13...Bd6; 14.Rxe6+ wins, because of 14...Qxe6; 15.Bxc6+ Bd7; 16.Bxa8 c6; 17.Qh5+ and Black cannot regain the piece without dropping more pawns, and may run into immediate devastation on the e-file.

14.Bxc6 Qxc6; 15.Nxd5.

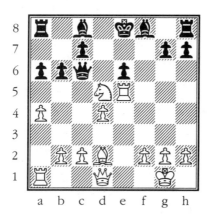

Black's position is a mess, but Petrosian manages to hang on somehow. **15...Bd7; 16.Bg5!** The Black king is choked and cannot flee. Survival will cost material.

16...Bd6; 17.Qh5+ Kf8. 17...g6 fails to 18.Qe2 Bxe5; 19.Qxe5 with a double attack at h8 and c7.

18.Qf3+ Kg8; 19.Rxe6.

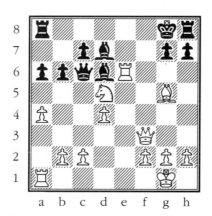

White has won two pawns and the attack is far from over. The game actually dragged out to the end of time control, which is rather surprising. **19...Rf8; 20.Ne7+ Bxe7; 21.Qxc6 Bxc6; 22.Rxe7** led to an endgame where the bishops of opposite colors stood in the way of immediate victory, though Geller did prevail in the end.

OVERLOADING

Overloading a piece means that the piece is given more defensive work than it can possibly handle. When a piece is overloaded, a simple decoy or deflection can remove it from the defense of a key square. You should always examine your opponent's pieces to see if any of them are overworked.

VASILY SMYSLOV VS. KOTOV
Moscow Championship, 1943

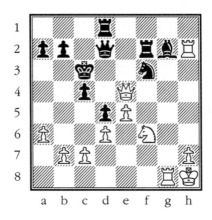

This is a position from our featured game by Smyslov. The rook at f7 is overloaded, having to defend both minor pieces. White won by capturing the bishop with the rook from h7, since if Black captures with the rook, then White picks off the knight at f6 with check, and the rook at g7 would also fall.

PROMOTION

Promoting a pawn to a queen is a central concept in the endgame. Usually the key to victory is getting the pawn to the last rank before the opponent manages to get a new queen. This concept is simple enough, but there are some twists, for example promoting to a piece other than the queen, which we will deal with a little later on.

BOBBY FISCHER VS. BERLINER
New York, 1960

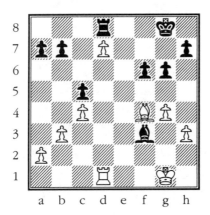

Promoting the pawn is White's goal. Fischer ignored the attack on his rook and played **36.Bc7.** Black resigned here, for if each side captures a rook, the White pawn cannot be prevented from promoting to a queen at d8.

Underpromotion

Never neglect the possibility of **underpromotion** (promoting a pawn to something other than a queen) as a tactic in the endgame. The underpromotion theme can be trivial and can be easy to overlook, or it can be buried deep in an artistic study. Underpromotion can involve replacing the pawn with a rook, bishop, or knight but only underpromotion to a knight, giving check, is common.

ROOK LIFT

The **rook lift** is a tactic which brings a rook into an attacking position by moving vertically up a rank, usually to the third rank, and then over to whichever file is most useful. The obvious advantages of the active rook sometimes inspires beginners to open the game by advancing a rook pawn two squares, just so the rook can be lifted. This is a faulty strategy, however, because early in the game the pivot squares at a3, h3, a6, and h6 are usually under the observation of enemy bishops. The rook lift should be used in the middlegame, not the opening. In our example, Steinitz falls victim to a rook lift tactic.

BLACKBURNE VS. WILHELM STEINITZ
London, 1883

23.Rd3! The entry of another rook into the attack along the third rank is decisive. **23...Rxe6; 24.Rh3 Qe7.** There is no defense to Qh6+ and Qxh7, e.g. 24...Re7; 25.Qh6+ Kg8; 26.Rhf3! Nb6; 27.Ne4.

25.Qh6+ Kg8; 26.Rf8+! Qxf8; 27.Qxh7#. A powerful demonstration of Blackburne's positional understanding and attacking skills.

The classic rook lift is illustrated in the next example, from a very famous game by Lasker.

EMANUEL LASKER VS. BAUER
Amsterdam, 1889

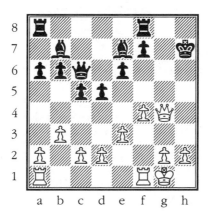

Lasker has sacrificed two pieces for a pair of pawns, but a rook lift wins the material back, and more.

19.Rf3 e5. The only defense. Now the Black queen can come to h6. **20. Rh3+ Qh6; 21. Rxh6+ Kxh6.**

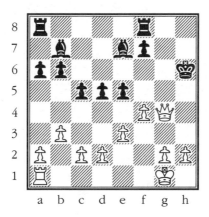

22. Qd7. This wins one of the bishops, and the game now is decisively in White's favor. **22...Bf6; 23.Qxb7.** and White won without difficulty.

8. PAUL MORPHY

Unofficial World Champion 1857–1859

American Paul Morphy was widely recognized as the best player of his time. A colorful figure, he was one of the most unique chess players in the history of the Royal Game. He demonstrated his skill against the best players in the world, then suddenly gave up the game and disappeared into obscurity.

During his brief career, he become a model for the following generation of chess players. His brilliant victories were published all over the world, and are still found in almost every introductory book. The game of chess has evolved and become much more sophisticated, but in the raw, unpolished games of the past century, we see instructive concepts in an easy to recognize form.

The title of World Champion had not been invented, and a number of candidates for unofficial World Champion have been considered for the period before Steinitz earned the first title in 1886. Morphy simply blew away the competition in the 1850s, dominating the game in a way that was not seen again for over a century, when another American soared to the top. So he is generally considered a genuine World Champion.

PAUL MORPHY VS. AN AMATEUR
New Orleans, 1858
Italian Game: Two Knights Defense
1.e4 e5; 2.Nf3 Nc6; 3.Bc4 Nf6; 4.d4.

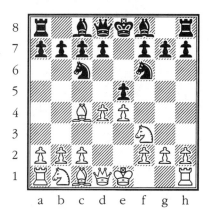

This approach to the Two Knight's Defense is a clearance operation, intended to get the Black pawn off of e5 so that White's pawn can advance.

4...exd4; 5.Ng5. A two-fold attack on f7. **5...d5.** A standard formula for reducing pressure on the diagonal. If White captures with the bishop, then Black can capture the bishop with the knight, eliminating the powerful attacker. 5...Ne5!? blocks the e-pawn, defends f7, and also attacks the bishop at c4, so what is wrong with it? Nothing, really. 6.Bb3 keeps up the pressure at f7, and White threatens to remove the defender with 7.f4. For example 6...h6; 7.f4.

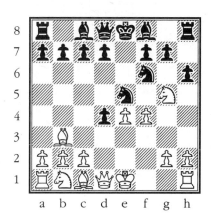

(7.Qxd4 Qe7 could lead to an interference tactic with 8.Ne6 fxe6; 9.Qxe5 with material equality, but 9...Qb4+ is a good reply since on 10.Nc3? Bd6; 11.Qb5 Nxe4, Black has won a pawn.) 7...hxg5; 8.fxe5 Nxe4; 9.Qxd4 Nc5; 10.Nc3 d6 and Black had the advantage in Pfleger vs. Spassky, Hastings 1965. Had Morphy tried his plan against Spassky, he might have been in for a rough ride!

6.exd5.

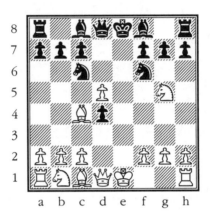

Later on players came to realize that Black had to play 6...Na5 here. Oddly, modern computers are inclined to take the pawn!

6...Nxd5. This loses, as Black's king becomes too exposed. Although there is a superficial resemblance to the Fegatello (Fried Liver) Attack, which is 4.Ng5 d5; 5.exd5 Nxd5; 6.Nxf7, here the open e-file is of great significance.

7.0–0 Be7.

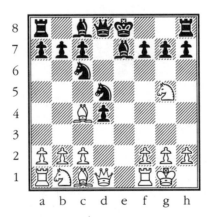

Black has no chance for survival now, as the White pieces close in for the kill.

8.Nxf7. The fork of the queen and rook forces Black to capture the knight. Part of the barrier has been destroyed, and Black's king will get dragged to e6 where it will shortly die of exposure.

8...Kxf7; 9.Qf3+.

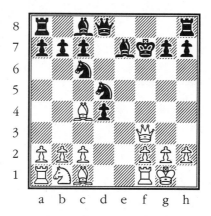

A double attack against the king and the knight at d5. **9...Ke6.**

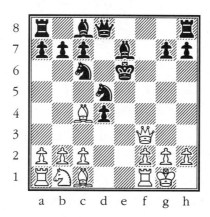

9...Ke8; 10.Bxd5 Ne5; 11.Qe4 still leaves Black in trouble on the e-file, and the castling privilege is forfeit. **10.Nc3.**

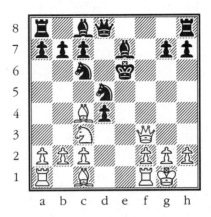

A deflection. Black's d-pawn is drawn away from its post, opeining up the d-file. Black can't decline, since d5 is under a three-fold attack.

10...dxc3; 11.Re1+ Ne5.

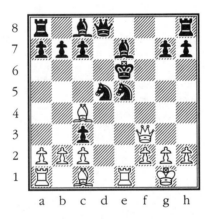

Computers usually don't appreciate the long term pressure that results from a pin. White plans to pile on with Bf4, and then doubling rooks on the e-file, or even sacrifice one rook at e5 to bring the other one to e1 quickly.

12.Bf4 Bf6; 13.Bxe5 Bxe5.

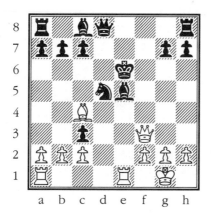

Black has two extra pieces, but they, the rooks, bishop and queen, do not participate in the defense. Powerful pins against the knight at d5 and bishop at e5 render the Black king helpless.

14.Rxe5+ Kxe5. Now it will be White's rook, queen and bishop against Black's bare king—not a fair fight.

15.Re1+ Kd4; 16.Bxd5.

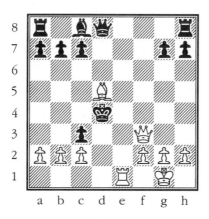

Black's king has nowhere to run.

16...Re8; 17.Qd3+ Kc5; 18.b4+. Not 18.Qxc3+ Kd6. Now 18...Kd6 allows 19.Bf3 mate. **18...Kxb4.** 18...Kb6; 19.Qd4+ Ka6; 20.b5+ leads to a mate similar to the game. **19.Qc4+.** Checkmate is now forced.

19...Ka5; 20.Qxc3+ Ka4; 21.Qb3+ Ka5; 22.Qa3+ Kb5; 23.Rb1#.

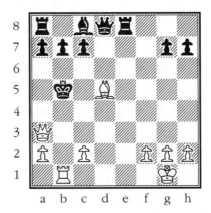

Black is finally checkmated. Impressed? Now consider that Morphy was playing six opponents in a simultaneous exhibition, and was blindfolded!

9. WILHELM STEINITZ

First Official World Champion (1886–1894)

Wilhelm Steinitz brought a scientific approach to the game of chess, and it is for this, as much as his victory in the first-ever World Championship match in 1886, that he is best remembered. Naturally he had a complete grasp of chess tactics, but his fundamental insight was that a game of chess should be won not by one great move but by the accumulation of small advantages.

Tactics were mere building blocks, materials out of which brilliant and elegant victories could be achieved. Calculation was paramount, and unlike Tal, Steinitz didn't make sacrifices on intuition. His games nevertheless contain many deep sacrifices as well as pure technical combinations.

Steinitz actually proclaimed himself World Champion back in 1866, when he defeated Adolf Anderssen, generally considered the finest player of the day once Paul Morphy stopped playing. It took twenty years before a consensus was reached in the matter. Steinitz reinforced his reputation with a large contribution to the chess literature, and his *Modern Chess Instructor* was a definitive manual on the game.

WILHELM STEINITZ VS. PILHAL
Vienna, 1862
Evans Gambit
1.e4 e5; 2.Nf3 Nc6; 3.Bc4 Bc5; 4.b4.

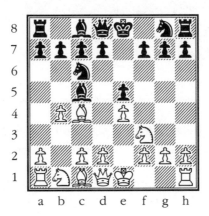

The Evans Gambit, launched with this move, involves a decoy. The bishop is brought to b4, where it can be attacked by a pawn.
4...Bxb4; 5.c3.

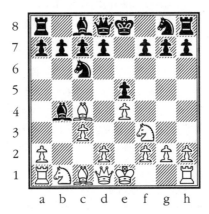

The immediate threat against the bishop is only part of the story. The move also prepares for an eventual advance of the d-pawn.

5...Ba5; 6.0–0 Nf6; 7.d4.

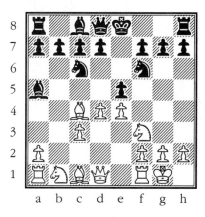

Black's pawn at d5 is under a double attack from the pawn and the knight.

7...exd4; 8.Ba3.

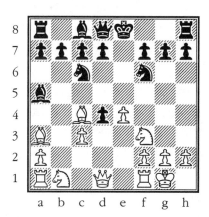

Steinitz applies a choke, depriving the enemy king of the crucial flight square to the kingside. Castling is now illegal.

8...d6. Black erects a barrier along the a3-f8 diagonal. **9.e5.** The pawn at e5 forks the knight at f6 and pawn at d6. White can now try to destroy the barrier at d6.

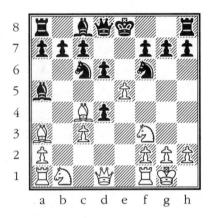

9...dxe5. 9...Nxe5 forks the bishop at c4 and knight at f3, but 10.Nxe5 dxe5; 11.Qb3 Qd7; 12.Re1 is strong, according to Russian analysis. Black has also tried 9...Ne4, 9...d5 and 9...Ng4, but none of these succeed in reducing White's pressure.

10.Qb3. The battery of queen and bishop threatens to destroy the pawn at f7. The king will have a hard time escaping. White has no other immediate threat, but this is enough to force Black into an awkward defense.

10...Qd7. On 10...Rf8 White could capture the enemy rook, but the bishop is stronger, and White can increase the pressure with 11.Ng5, renewing the threat at f7. The knight also attacks the pawn at h7, a small fork. The h-pawn is defended, of course. Still, it means that the knight at f6 is paralyzed, required to defend the pawn. 11...Qd7; 12.Re1 dxc3; 13.Nxc3 Bxc3; 14.Qxc3 leaves White three pawns down, but Black is already lost. The threat is the removal of the defender of the rook at f8. If the king is forced to move to the d-file, then White can capture the rook for free.

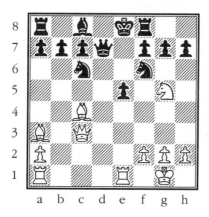

The Black rook at f8 and pawns at e5, f7, and h7 are under attack. Each is defended, for the moment, but White can play Bb4, pinning the knight which is the only defender of the e-pawn which is an important defender of the e-file. The sacrifice of three pawns turns out to be justified. 14...Nd4; 15.Rxe5+ Ne6 defends against previous threats, but the e6-square is attacked by three pieces, and another rook can come to the e-file. 16.Rae1 increases the pressure on the e-file, and Black has no defense, for example 16...Qd8, which lends the support of the bishop to e6, loses because White can add even more fuel to the fire with 17.Qh3.

This is a double attack on the pawn at e6 and pawn at h7. The knight at e6 is attacked by five pieces, and defended only by two. Black's position quickly falls apart, for example 17...h6 is mated in seven moves.

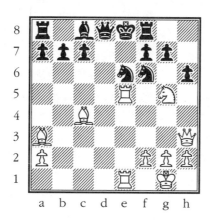

18.Bxe6 Qe7; 19.Bd7+. The discovered attack on the Black queen is combined with a check, but this is not a discovered check, because in that requires a piece which was not moved to give check. 19...Bxd7; 20.Rxe7+ Kd8; 21.Qxd7+! A queen sacrifice sets up a finish where the knight at g5 delivers the final blow.

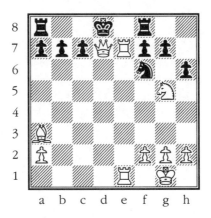

21...Nxd7; 22.Nxf7+. Deflection. (Or 22.Re8+, which deflects the rook from the defense of e7, while also decoying it to a square where it will be captured. 22...Rxe8; 23.Nxf7+ Kc8; 24.Rxe8#.) 22...Kc8 (22...Rxf7; 23.Re8#.); 23.Re8+ Rxe8; 24.Rxe8#. Returning to the game, we see that Black's choice, capturing at e5 with the pawn, restores the choke, as the king can no longer cross f8.

11.Re1.

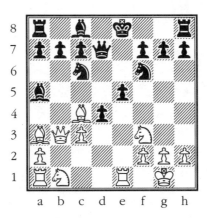

The pin on the e-file weakens support of d4, and creates long-term threats against the enemy king.

11...Qf5; 12.Bb5!

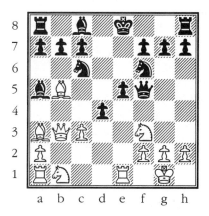

Another pin, this time against the knight which is supporting the e-pawn. White threatens 13.Rxe5+, winning the queen.

12...Nd7. An ugly move, but the pin must be broken and the pawn at e5 requires additional support. **13.Qd5.** This fine move adds pressure to e5 and c6 simultaneously.

13...Bxc3; 14.Nxc3 dxc3.

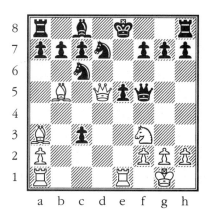

Although the pawn at e5 is defended by three pieces and attacked by three pieces, it is actually lost because whenever one of the Black knights move, the pin on the other knight will be reactivated.

15.Nxe5 Ne7; 16.Nxd7!

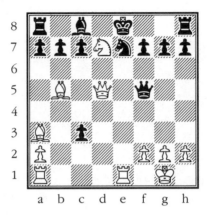

This is a discovered attack against the Black queen. Of course the queen can now capture its undefended White counterpart, but there are more tactics in store.

16...Qxd5. Black would be checkmated in any case. The most prolonged suffering would be 16...c6; 17.Rxe7+ Kd8; 18.Qxf5 cxb5; 19.Nb6!! Bxf5; 20.Rd1+ Bd3; 21.Rxd3#.

17.Nf6+.

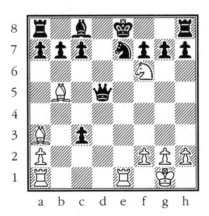

Forking the king and queen. **17...Kf8; 18.Bxe7#.**

10. EMANUEL LASKER

Second World Champion (1894–1921)

Lasker built on Steinitz's positional understanding but was in many respects quite a different player. Lasker was a very practical player. For him, psychological aspects of the game were as important as mathematical calculations. He did not attempt to storm the enemy position quickly as did Morphy or, later, Tal, but rather waited for an opportunity to take advantage of an enemy mistake. He had an almost inexhaustible patience, and was quite content to play a long waiting game hoping to bore his enemy into blundering.

Sharp tactics and a keen eye for weaknesses in the enemy position usually brought Lasker victory. He managed to hold onto the world championship title for 27 years, a record that remains unbroken. Indeed, it is unlikely that any modern world champion will be able to retain supremacy for such a long period of time.

Lasker's games resemble many modern contests played on the weekend tournament circuit. Modern masters employ the same patient waiting game, confident that inferior opposition will sooner or later make a critical mistake which will allow resolution of the game by tactical means.

EMANUEL LASKER VS. MARSHALL
St. Petersburg International, Russia, 1914
Russian Game
1.e4 e5; 2.Nf3 Nf6; 3.Nxe5 d6; 4.Nf3 Nxe4; 5.Qe2.

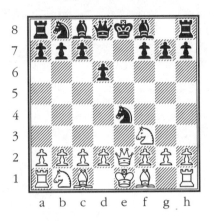

This variation of the Russian Game features a pin on the e-file. It is not considered very strong, because Black can arrange for an early exchange of queens and head for a level endgame. Lasker, always a practical competitor, knew that the swashbuckling Marshall was unlikely to follow this course.

5...Qe7; 6.d3 Nf6; 7.Bg5.

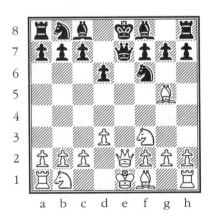

The pin against the knight is not very significant because Black could easily release the tension by exchanging queens.

7...Be6?! Stubbornly keeping queens on. 7...Qxe2+; 8.Bxe2 Be7 would have been tediously equal. **8.Nc3 Nbd7; 9.0-0-0 h6.** The advance of the h-pawn and g-pawn is a standard method for combating a pin. The bishop is driven back to g3, but Black accepts a weakened kingside. In this game, the weakness of the kingside is not critical, as both sides are castling queenside.

10.Bh4 g5; 11.Bg3.

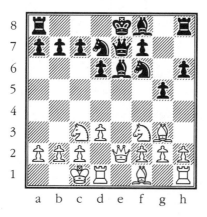

The pin has been broken, and for the moment there are no tactical threats. Marshall could safely castle here, but since the bishop at g3 is trapped, decides to eliminate it.

11...Nh5; 12.d4 Nxg3; 13.hxg3. There is a small pin here. The pawn at h6 cannot leave the h-file since then the rook at h8 would be lost. Although g5 is also defended by the queen, Marshall decides to advance the g-pawn. **13...g4?!**

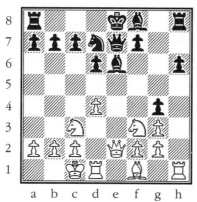

Too ambitious.

14.Nh4. Retreating to d2 would have been much wiser. After all, the queenside is going to be the arena, and this horse has wandered far away. Fortunately for Lasker, he doesn't need it. **14...d5?** Marshall wanted to prevent the advance of White's e-pawn, which would have driven away the bishop and allowed an exchange of queens, which is unfavorable for Black now that the kingside pawn structure is weakened. 14...Nb6 was suggested by Tarrasch; 15.d5 Bd7; 16.Qxe7+ Bxe7 is not too bad for Black, despite the kingside pawn structure weakness, because Black has the bishop pair as compensation.

15.Qb5! This is a double attack, because in addition to the vulnerable pawn at b7, Black must also worry about the threat of Nxd5. The tactic is used to bring the queen to the queenside, where the future battle will take place.

15...0–0–0; 16.Qa5. The queen attacks vulnerable points at a7, c7 and d5. Only Qxa7 is a threat, however. If White were to foolishly grab the d-pawn with the knight, then Black has ...Qg5+!

16...a6.

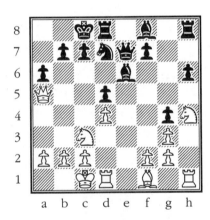

17.Bxa6. Destruction of the barrier. The sacrifice is not really part of a combination, but is more of an investment. No forced win is immediately evident, but the weak position of the Black king must be exploited sooner or later.

17...bxa6; 18.Qxa6+ Kb8; 19.Nb5.

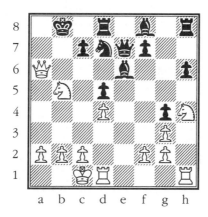

The knight attacks both a7 and c7, and the c3-square is cleared so that a rook can join the attack on the third rank.

19...Nb6; 20.Rd3. This is a rook lift. Rooks often travel horizontally along the third rank.

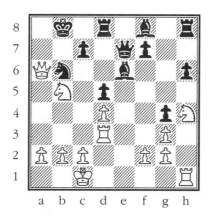

20...Qg5+. 20...Nc4; 21.Re1 sets an important pin on the e-file. (21.Rb3 Qg5+; 22.Kb1 Nd2+ forks the king and rook, and worse, the rook will fall with check. 23.Ka1 Nxb3+; 24.cxb3 Bd6. White has insufficient attacking material.) 21...Rd6. (21...Qg5+ doesn't work now. 22.Kb1 Bd6; 23.Rxe6! fxe6; 24.Na7. White has the mating threat Nc6#.) 22.Qa7+ Kc8; 23.Nf5! This fork is made possible by the pin on the e-file. 23...Qg5+; 24.Kb1 Rc6; 25.Qa8+ Kd7; 26.Na7 has a mating threat of Qc8, and also attacks the rook. After

26...Qxf5; 27.Qxc6+ Kd8; 28.Re2 White has a material advantage and threatens Rb3.

21.Kb1 Bd6; 22.Rb3. Lasker sets up a pin against the knight at b6. **22...Rhe8; 23.a4 Bf5; 24.Na7.** Threatening a fork at c6. **24...Bd7.**

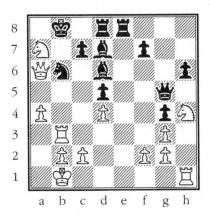

25.a5. The pin is exploited with the assistance of the a-pawn. **25...Qd2; 26.axb6 Re1+; 27.Ka2.** There is no need to worry about the rook at h1.

27...c6.

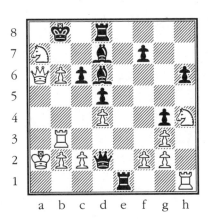

28.Nb5! Deflection. Facing the threat of 29.Qa7+ and subsequent checkmate Marshall decides to grab the knight.

28...cxb5. 28...Rh8; 29.Nxd6 was another way to go down. **29.Qa7+.**

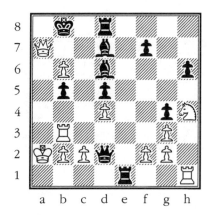

Black resigned, because of 29...Kc8; 30.b7+ Kc7; 31.b8Q+ when the pawn promotes with discovered double check! 31...Kc6; 32.Qab6#.

11. JOSE RAUL CAPABLANCA

Third World Champion (1921–1927)

Jose Raoul Capablanca y Graupera, often referred to simply as "Capa" got off to a fast start, winning the Cuban Championship at the age of 12. He is better remembered however as a technician. Capablanca had an ability to exploit small positional advantages very effectively, often reaching endgames where his superior technique brought victory. He worked very hard at the game. His study of rook and pawn end games was extremely thorough.

Nevertheless, Capablanca's games show tactical brilliance in abundance. Sometimes his combinations were used for direct attack, but more often he employed tactical means to reduce the position to bring about a winning endgame. Capablanca liked simplicity, and his tactics were often pure yet elegant.

JOSE CAPABLANCA VS. ZUBAREV
Moscow Internatonal, 1925
Queen's Gambit Accepted

1.d4 d5; 2.c4 e6; 3.Nf3 dxc4. An old move order to reach the Queen's Gambit Accepted, one which is returning to favor these days.

4.e4 c5; 5.d5 exd5; 6.exd5 Nf6; 7.Bxc4 Bd6; 8.0-0 0-0; 9.Bg5 Bg4; 10.Nc3 Nbd7.

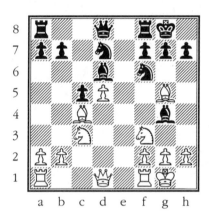

Both sides have developed the majority of their pieces. Each has pinned an enemy knight to a queen. It is White's turn to move, however, and Capablanca uses a fork to put more pressure on the knight at f6.

11.Ne4 Qc7? A terrible move. If White captures the bishop at d6, then Black has blockaded the weak d-pawn and has chances to win it. Capablanca has no interest in that exchange, however. Instead, he gives up the bishop pair to damage the pawn barrier protecting Black's king. 11...Be5 is correct. The bishop cannot be captured because the knight at f3 is pinned. 12.Nxe5 Bxd1; 13.Nxd7 Qxd7; 14.Bxf6 gets two pieces for the queen, but that is not enough. Black would retreat the bishop from d1 to a safer square on the kingside. Of course, Black would not fall for 14...gxf6; 15.Nxf6+ with a fork that results in an extra piece and pawn.

12.Bxf6 Nxf6. 12...Bxh2+ is an intermezzo that fails after 13.Kh1 Nxf6. Some commentators have suggested 14.d6 but that is a mistake because after 14...Qd8; 15.Nxf6+ (15.Nxc5 Qxd6; 16.Qxd6 Bxd6; 17.Nxb7 is relatively better, but 17...Bf4 is better for Black, who has the bishop pair) 15...Qxf6; 16.Kxh2, there is a fork. 16...Qf4+ wins the bishop at c4, and Black retains a one pawn advantage. 14.Nxf6+! is best.

13.Nxf6+ gxf6.

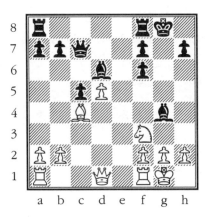

Black threatens 14...Bxh2+, because the knight at f3 is pinned. **14.h3.** White not only saves the pawn at h2, but also drives back the pinning bishop. **14...Bh5; 15.Re1 Rfe8; 16.Qb3.** The pin is broken at last.

16...a6; 17.a4 Bg6; 18.Bd3. This move is primarily a clearance, liberating c4 for use by the knight, which can get there via d2. White has no intention of exchanging at g6, which would allow Black to repair the damage to the kingside pawn structure.

18...Qd7?! 18...Rad8 was more logical. 18...Bf4 is another reasonable try, taking d2 away from the knight. **19.Nd2 Re7.**

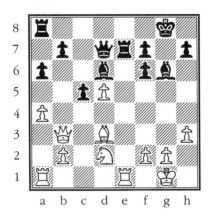

Black plans to double rooks on the e-file, taking control of critical squares. White's rooks can be used to attack weak pawns, using a rook lift at e3, so it makes sense to try to get them off the board. 19...Rxe1+; 20.Rxe1 Bxd3; 21.Qxd3 Qxa4 wins a pawn, but 22.Nc4 threatens a fork at b6, as well as the bishop at d6. Black can play 22...Qb5, pinning the knight. White defends the queen with 23.Re3, renewing the threat of Nxd6, and lifting the rook to the third rank where it can work on the kingside. The bishop is overworked, because it must block the pawn, guard g3, and support c5. If it retreats to c7, White can cut off the diagonal by advancing the d-pawn to d6.

20.Bxg6 fxg6. 20...hxg6; 21.Ne4 is similar, but even worse for Black because of 21...Kg7; 22.Qf3 f5; 23.Nxc5! Bxc5 and the fork 24.Qc3+ regains the piece with a pawn advantage. 24...Kg8; 25.Qxc5 Rxe1+; 26.Rxe1 Qxa4 picks up the pawn but allows the deadly infiltration 27.Qe7, and the d-pawn will be escorted to d8. 27...Qa5; 28.d6 Rd8; 29.Rc1! The interference move 30.Rc7 is threatened, when pawns at f7 and b7 will also be under attack.

21.Ne4.

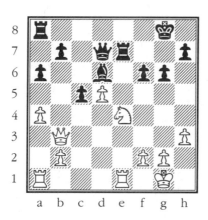

White has improved Black's pawn structure, but Capablanca has a deadly threat of a fork at f6. The knight at e4 forks the f-pawn, the c-pawn and the bishop at d6. The bishop is now blocking the passed d-pawn, and Black would prefer to hang on to it. But the bishop is the only defender of the pawn at c5! Even though the bishop and pawn are defended, the fork lays the groundwork for additional tactics.

21...Kg7; 22.Qc3. The weakling at f6 is now pinned. Black has nothing better than to use the bishop to defend it, leaving the pawn at c5 defenseless.

22...Be5.

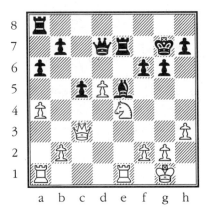

The queen and bishop are skewered, so Black will regain the pawn. **23.Qxc5 Bxb2; 24.Ng5.**

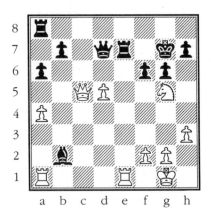

A discovered attack on the rook at e7 allows the knight to gain entrance to e6.

24...Rae8; 25.Ne6+ Kf7; 26.Rab1 Be5.

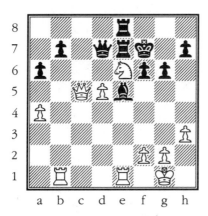

This has control of greater space and a passed pawn, but the winning strategy is not simple. With the e-file blocked, one might be tempted to double rooks on the b-file which runs into a nasty pin, so Capablanca found a better plan.

27.Qc4. 27.Rb6 Bc7 works because the knight is pinned on the e-file. If 28.Rxb7?! Black wins the exchange with 28...Bh2+, a discovered attack. 29.Kxh2 Qxb7.

27...Rc8; 28.Qb3.

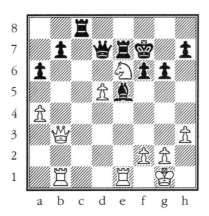

28...Bb8. 28...Rc3 should be met by retreating the queen to a2. The tempting 29.Qxb7? Qxb7; 30.Rxb7 Rxb7; 31.Nd8+ Kg7; 32.Nxb7 amounts to nothing after 32...Rd3, for example 33.Nc5 Rxd5; 34.Nxa6 Ra5 and the a-pawn drops.

29.g3 Qd6; 30.Nf4! Capablanca clears e6 for use by the rook. **30...Rce8; 31.Re6!**

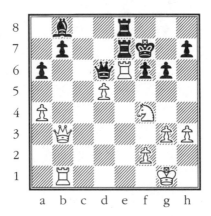

The rook attacks the queen, rook and f-pawn simultaneously. The blockader of the d-pawn is driven back, since Black can hardly afford to exchange at e6.

31...Qd7. 31...Rxe6; 32.dxe6+ Kg7; 33.Qxb7+ with Qd7 to follow. **32.Rxe7+!** New circumstances require new tactics. The rook accomplished its mission by clearing d6. Now the d-pawn can advance with discovered check.

32...Kxe7. 32...Rxe7; 33.d6+ wins too much material. **33.Qxb7!** White attacks both queen and a-pawn. The knight at f4 is vulnerable, and Black quickly takes advantage of an opportunity to get rid of it.

33...Bxf4; 34.Re1+.

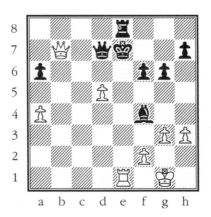

This may have come as a surprising intermezzo because Black can retreat the bishop to the relative safety of e5. 34.gxf4 Qxb7; 35.Rxb7+ Kd6; 36.Rxh7 Re4 gives Black excellent drawing chances.

34...Be5; 35.d6+! Because the bishop and queen are pinned, Black must use the king to capture the d-pawn. That would place the king on the same file as the queen, and White would play Rd1+, x-raying the king to get at the Black queen. The decoy must be left alone. Even so, it achieves a goal, clearing the a2-g8 diagonal.

35...Ke6; 36.Qb3+ Kf5. The only legal move. **37.Qd3+.**

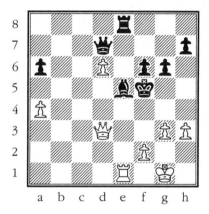

37...Kg5. 37...Ke6; 38.Qc4+ Kf5?? (38...Kxd6 transposes to the game.) 39.Qg4#. **38.Qe3+ Kf5; 39.Qe4+.** 39.g4+ Ke6; 40.Qb3+ would have been a little faster. **39...Ke6; 40.Qc4+ Kxd6; 41.Rd1+.** The x-ray wraps things up quicky.

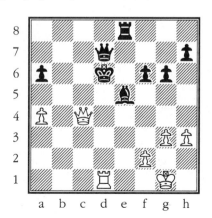

41...Ke7; 42.Rxd7+ Kxd7. Black's rook and bishop are no match for the queen. **43.Qxa6 Rb8; 44.Qa7+ Kc6; 45.Qxh7 Rb2; 46.Qxg6.** Black resigned.

12. ALEXANDER ALEKHINE

Fourth World Champion (1927–1935 and 1937–1946)

Alekhine has long been associated with chess tactics. His collection of best games has been studied by most advanced chess players, including many world champions. These games never fail to include sparkling tactical maneuvers. Although Alekhine was formidable in all aspects of the game, he was most fearsome as a tactician.

Alekhine's is tactical prowess kept him at the top of the chess world for most of the period between the two world wars. Even if he fell into a poor position, a trap, swindle, or combination would turn the tide. Even his endgames could be highly tactical. Not many of his opponents were able to survive until the final stage of the game. Alekhine cut them down in the middle game using maximally effective attacks combining a variety of tactics.

The vast legacy of tactical lessons taught by Alekhine remains available in the many collections devoted to his games. Simply playing through each of the games carefully is a fine lesson in the art of tactics as well as a rich and rewarding chess experience. Here is one of his best achievements.

ALEXANDER ALEKHINE VS. MAROCZY
International Chess Tournament, Bled, 1931
Queen's Gambit Declined

This game is particularly fascinating for several reasons. Long considered a classic, it has been commented on by many scholars, and the players themselves. Yet even after almost 70 years, some of the tactics have still not been properly described and evaluated. We take some pleasure in presenting our revisionist view here, with the usual caveat that there may be even more to be discovered.

1.d4 d5; 2.c4 e6; 3.Nc3 Nf6; 4.Bg5 Be7; 5.e3 Nbd7; 6.Nf3 0-0; 7.Rc1 h6; 8.Bh4 c6; 9.Bd3 a6; 10.0-0 dxc4; 11.Bxc4 c5?!; 12.a4 Qa5; 13.Qe2 cxd4; 14.exd4 Nb6.

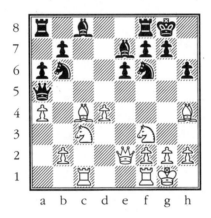

The opening has followed the path of the stodgy old Orthodox Defense to the Queen's Gambit. White has an isolated pawn at d4, which is somewhat weak but also offeres tactical possiblities. Maroczy has attacked the a-pawn with both knight and queen. Alekhine makes no effort to save it, but goes instead for an attack. Alekhine had the luxury of a 5-point lead after 23 rounds of the supertournament, and could afford to take chances.

15.Bd3! Bd7. 15...Nxa4; 16.Nxa4 (Alekhine preferred 16.Ne4 which threatens to remove important defenders of the kingside and also destroy, or at least weaken, the pawn barrier protecting the Black king, but the position after 16...Nd5; 17.Bxe7 Nxe7 remains unclear.) 16...Qxa4; 17.Rc7 is very good for White, who can even afford to sacrifice the exchange with 17...Bd6; 18.Bxf6 since 18...gxf6; 19.Qe3 Kg7. (19...Bxc7? is again wrong because of

20.Qxh6 f5; 21.Ng5 and mate cannot be avoided.) Even worse is 18...Bxc7? 19.Qe4 sets up a mating threat that can only be defended by 19...g6 but then 20.Qh4 h5; 21.Qg5 wins. **16.Ne5.**

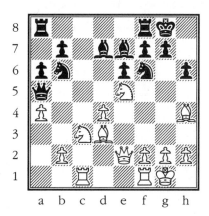

The mating threat of exchanging at f6 followed by Qe4 remains in force.

16...Rfd8. The a-pawn is still taboo. 16...Bxa4; 17.Bxf6 Bxf6; 18.Qe4 Rfd8 gives the Black king an escape path via f8, but White has a surprising resource on the other side of the board, 19.b4! Decoy or deflection? At first it is hard to see the point of the pawn sacrifice. The key is actually the infiltration of the rook to the seventh rank at c7. However, there are holes in the traditional analysis. 19...Qxb4; 20.Qh7+ Kf8; 21.Nxa4.

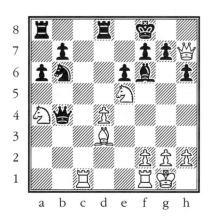

This is a fascinating position. Commentators have stopped here, assuming that White will get a rook to c7 after the knight at a4 is taken. Black has a way of complicating matters which has so far gone unnoticed. 21...Bxe5! The bishop removes one of the attackers and simultaneously guards c7! (21...Nxa4; 22.Rc7 leads to checkmate.) 22.Nxb6 qualifies as a desperado, but there are plenty of desperate characters here, and Black responds in kind.

22...Bxh2+!; 23.Kxh2 Qxb6. Black is down a piece, but has three pawns. 24.Qh8+ Ke7; 25.Qxg7 Rxd4 and White cannot play 26.Rb1 because of 26...Qd6+, winning the bishop.

17.f4!?

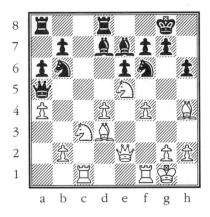

White would have liked to exploit the pin with Ng4 immediately, but Maroczy had planned 17.Ng4 Nfd5; 18.Nxd5 Nxd5; 19.Bxe7 Nxe7 and there are enough Black pieces to defend the king.

17...Be8; 18.Ng4! Typical Alekhine, sacrificing a pawn for the attack. **18...Rxd4.** Accepting the sacrifice is risky, but how could Black decline, when the alternatives seemed so dangerous? 18...Nxg4; 19.Bxe7 Rd7; 20.Bc5! White wins a piece, because the knight at g4 cannot retreat, as then the Black queen suffers the fate of a trapped piece after, 21.b4! 18...Nbd5; 19.Nxd5 Nxd5. (19...Rxd5; 20.Bxf6 Bxf6; 21.Nxf6+ gxf6 destroys the pawn barrier and White can use the interference, 22.f5 to cut off the Black queen and rook from the defense. Black would be in serious trouble.) 20.Qe4 has been suggested as giving White a strong position, but how much compensation does White really have after 20...Bxh4; 21.Qh7+ Kf8?

19.Bxf6 Bxf6; 20.Nxf6+ gxf6; 21.Ne4!

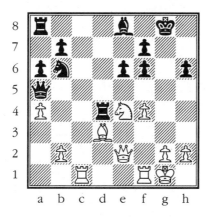

The pawn barrier has been weakened, and f6 is now the focus of White's attention. We can see a variety of tactical themes at work. There is the threat of a fork at f6, and a rook lift is available on either the c-file or f-file to bring additional force to bear. The advance of White's f-pawn can be used to create a block and an interference simultaneously.

21...Rad8? 21...Nd7 allows the powerful blow 22.f5! This is a block, and interference, and in some sense a clearance because the opening of the f-file is an additional goal. 22...e5 keeps things closed but also cuts off all of Black's pieces, except the knight at d7, from the defense of the king. (22...exf5; 23.Ng3 keeps the Black king in a state of perpetual nervousness, and the f-pawns may fall quickly.) 23.Rf3 is a strong reply. True, Black's king can evacuate via f8, but then the pawn at h6 will eventually fall and the White h-pawn will have a clear vista to the promotion square. 23...Qxa4; 24.Rg3+ Kf8; 25.Nxf6! Nxf6; 26.Qxe5.

The sacrifice of the knight clears the e-file and the Black king cannot escape. Black has an extra piece, but can't hold on to it. 26...Ng4; 27.Qh8+ Ke7; 28.h3 rounds up the knight. 21...f5 is the correct defense. Alekhine would have had to find the most precise continuation, worked out by analysts as 22.Nc5, threatening a fork with Nb3.

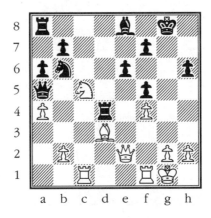

22...Qb4. (22...Bxa4; 23.Rf3 and if the king tries to run wth 23...Kf8 White can try the sacrifice 24.Nxe6+ forking king and rook, so acceptance is mandatory. 24...fxe6; 25.Qxe6 threatening Rc7 and Rg3, each with deadly threats.) 23.Qe5 (23.Nxe6 fxe6; 24.Qxe6+ Bf7; 25.Qxf5 Rd6 and Black survives.) 23...Nd5 was the only moved considered by the analysis, but (23...Rd5 also comes into consideration, for example 24.Qe3 Nxa4 and here one has to be rather skeptical of 25.Nxe6 fxe6; 26.Qxe6+ Bf7 because the bishop at d3 hangs.) 24.Rf3 was shown to be a strong reply, though Black may be able to hang in with 24...Nxf4; 25.Rg3+ Kf8; 26.Qg7+ (26.Bxf5 is just ignored with 26...Rad8 when it is Black who has attacking chances.) 26...Ke7; 27.Qxh6 Bc6!

Perhaps Alekhine's conception turns out to be flawed, or perhaps we have missed something and future analysts will rehabilitate the variation. Time will tell.

22.Nxf6+ Kf8.

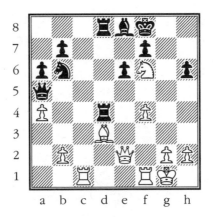

Black's king is a little vulnerable, but it is not easy to see how the attack can be furthered. The tactics really fly now! 22...Kh8 has been dismissed unfairly. 23.Qg4 threatens mate at g8, so Black must move the bishop. 23...Bc6! (23...Bxa4; 24.Qh4 also allows the same defense, and here it is even stronger. 24...Qg5! taking advantage of the pin on the pawn at f4. 25.fxg5 Rxh4; 26.Be4 Bb5!?; 27.Rf2 hxg5; 28.g3 Rh6; 29.Ng4 Rh5; 30.Rxf7 and the rook can still be trapped with Bg6.) 24.Qh4 Qg5! gives Black a good game. 25.fxg5 Rxh4; 26.g6 fxg6; 27.Bxg6 Rxa4 leaves White a pawn down with nothing to show for it.

23.Nh7+! The direct attack commences. There are no pins, forks, skewers in sight, but underlying the attack is a whole series of instructive diversions, interferences and other tactics.

23...Ke7. 23...Kg8; 24.Qg4+ Kh8; 25.Qh4 h5! (25...Rxd3; 26.Qxh6 is deadly.) 26.Qf6+ Kg8; 27.b4! is a premonition of what takes place in the game. 27...Qd5 takes away d5 from the Black knight, and 28.Qe7 Qd6; 29.Qg5+ leads to mate in two, now that the queen has left the fifth rank. **24.f5 R8d6.**

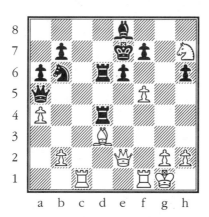

24...Rxd3 loses to 25.f6+! An intereference is used. The Black king is forced to the d-file, so the rook at d3 falls with check **25.b4!** White could not launch the attack immediately with 25.Qh5 because of 15...Qd2!

25...Qxb4. Or, as Alekhine demonstrated, 25...Rxb4; 26.Qh5 e5. Necessary, as otherwise the pawn gets to f6 with check and a discovered attack against the enemy queen. 27.f6+! Kd8; 28.Qxh6! Alekhine would willingly part with the bishop to get access to f8.

28...Rxd3; 29.Qf8 Rd7. It is clear now why the other rook had to be deflected from the d-file, where it could assist in the defense. 30.Rc5! White interferes with the Black queen's path to a defensive post at d5. In addition, should the knight eventually move, it cuts off a check from b6.

Finally, it deflects the queen. 30...Qxa4; 31.Rxe5 Rc7. A discovered defense! The bishop is protected by the queen at a4. 32.Rfe1 wins the pinned bishop.

26.Qe5. White spins a mating web, with f6+ and Nf8# threatened. **26...Nd7.** 26...Rc6; 27.Rxc6 Bxc6; 28.fxe6 fxe6; 29.Bg6! Nd7; 30.Qc7 has been considered winning for White, as Rf7 is coming. What has been overlooked, however, is that the rook at f1 can be pinned! 30...Rd1. Black now threatens to remove the defender with ...Qc5+, so White must capture the rook. 31.Rxd1.

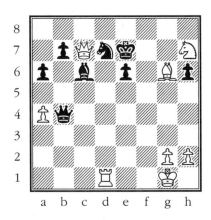

The analysts fail to see a big discovered attack coming. 31...Qc5+; 32.Kh1 Bxg2+!; 33.Kxg2 Qxc7. Black has a decisive material advantage.

27.Qh8. A different mate is looming: f6+ followed by Qxe8#. **27...Rxd3?** 27...Rc6 is the best defense as suggested by Maroczy. 28.Rxc6 bxc6; 29.fxe6 fxe6; 30.Nf6! Nxf6; 31.Qxf6+ Kd7; 32.Qxh6 Qxa4 (32...Rxd3?; 33.Qh7+); 33.Bxa6. The bishop cannot be captured because then White will fork at g7, grabbing the rook.

White has a more secure king, connected passed pawns, and a better bishop, which should be enough of an advantage to win. 27...Qb6 sets up a discovered check, but 28.a5! puts a stop to that plan.

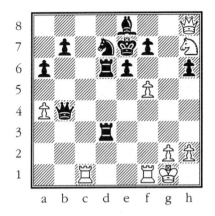

28.f6+. Alekhine announced mate in two.

28...Kd8. 28...Nxf6; 29.Qxf6+ Kd7; 30.Nf8#. **29.Qxe8+!** The decoy completes the tactical devastation. **29...Kxe8; 30.Rc8#.**

13. MAX EUWE

Fifth World Champion (1935–1937)

The next world champion, Euwe, is better known as an author of definitive books than as a chess champion. He won the title from Alekhine in 1935 in a match where the champion is reported to have been drinking pretty heavily. An early lead in the match led to complacency and Alekhine's play deteriorated. The Challenger was better prepared in this match but two years later Alekhine reclaimed the title in a more serious encounter which wasn't even close.

Euwe was capable of exceptionally brilliant play. His attacks were light thunderstorms, raining down on the enemy position. Deeply calculated combinations can be found in many of his games. This game was the 12th in the 1935 match for the World Championship. Alekhine, defending his title, had a comfortable lead early on, but Euwe had closed the gap and needed a victory to pull even.

MAX EUWE VS. ALEXANDER ALEKHINE
World Championship Match, 12th Game, Holland, 1935
Gruenfeld Defense

1.d4 Nf6; 2.c4 g6; 3.Nc3 d5; 4.Qb3 dxc4; 5.Qxc4 Bg7; 6.e4 0–0; 7.Nf3 a6; 8.Bf4!?

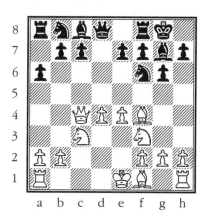

This approach to the Hungarian Variation of the Gruenfeld Defense is quite rare these days, because 8.e5 is normally seen.

8...b5. A bit rash. The odd-looking 8...c6 is considered stronger. **9.Qxc7.** The idea behind this strange sacrifice is that the White queen may become trapped, lacking any clear escape path.

9...Qe8. 9...b4 undermines the support of e4 but allows the knight to get into the attack after 10.Na4 Nxe4; 11.Nb6 when Black must lose material. **10.Be2 Nc6.** Will the queen become a trapped piece? That is certainly Alekhine's intention. **11.d5 Nb4.** Threatening a fork at c2.

12.0–0.

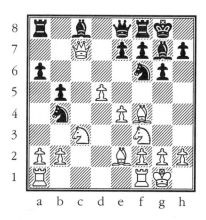

Black gets two pawns and the initiative for a knight with an ambitious sacrifice, but will it be enough? Black was already down a pawn.

12...Nxe4!?; 13.Nxe4 Nxd5; 14.Qc1.

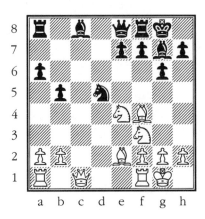

At the moment, Black has just a single pawn for the piece. The pawn at b2 is pinned, and perhaps the e-pawn and f-pawn can be advanced. Black can develop quickly, and if the rook at a1 can be kept out of play, would have some compensation.

14...Bf5?! The obvious move, but capturing at f4, removing the defender of the b-pawn, would have been wiser. 14...Nxf4!; 15.Qxf4 Bxb2; 16.Rad1 Bg7 would have provided more counterplay. Two pawns, the bishop pair and a central pawnroller are not quite worth a piece, but at this point Black is just looking to maximize chances in a desperate situation.

15.Ng3 Rc8; 16.Qd2 Nxf4; 17.Qxf4 Bc2. White's rooks are now active, and taking the b-pawn is out of the question because of the double-attack on the bishop at f5. 17...Bxb2; 18.Nxf5 and now 18...Bxa1; 19.Nh6+ gives White three pieces for a rook and two pawns. 19.Qh6 forces mate, the main threat being Ng5 and Qxh7#. Instead, Black can try18...gxf5, but White has 19.Rab1 followed by the win of the f-pawn and probably a mating attack in the near future. Once the bishop retreats, a rook lift via b3 is possible.

18.Qb4!

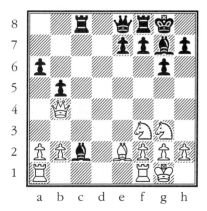

White uses the mighty queen to defend the lowly pawn, but it is worth it.

18...Qd8; 19.Ne1. Euwe is willing to retreat and maneuver as needed to hang on to his pawns. The pieces will re-emerge to take up attacking positions a little later.

19...Ba4; 20.Rb1. Finally, the pin is broken. **20...Bd4.**

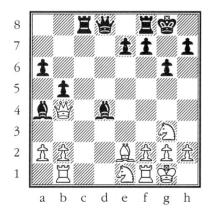

This sets a little trap involving a trapped piece.

21.Nf3! 21.b3 entombs the bishop at a4, but Black has 21...a5!; 22.Qa3 (22.Qd2? loses the queen to a discovered attack: 22...Bxf2+!) 22...Bc5; 23.b4!? (23.Qb2 Bd4 repeating the position and earning a draw; 23.Qc1 Bxf2+; 24.Rxf2 Rxc1; 25.Rxc1 was an acceptable alternative, since the bishop at a4 is trapped. After 25...Qd2; 26.Rd1

Qxa2; 27.bxa4 Qxa4 White has a rook and three pieces for a queen and four pawns. The pawns are healthy, and Black has enough counterplay to render a verdict on the position difficult.) 23...Bxb4; 24.Qe3 Qd5 and Black has significant counterplay.

21...Bc5; 22.Qh4! White's Queen returns to an active position. **22...Bc2; 23.Rbc1.**

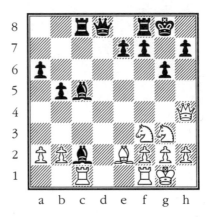

23...f6. Since the bishop at c2 has nowhere to run, Alekhine tries to save some material by tactical means. **24.Bc4!** The bishop uses the interference and double attack tactics simultaneously. Black must capture, but White gets to give a check which buys time to grab the bishop at c2. 24.Rxc2 gives Black the discovered check 24...Bxf2+; 25.Rxf2 Rxc2 though White is still winning after 26.Qe4.

24...bxc4; 25.Qxc4+ Kg7; 26.Qxc2.

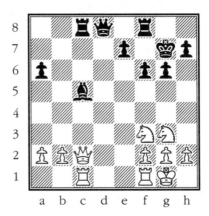

26...Qa5. 26...Bxf2+ doesn't work anymore, because White can just capture with the queen. **27.Qe2 e5.** 27...Qxa2; 28.Rxc5 Rxc5; 29.Qxe7+ is a triple attack that wins a rook. **28.a3.** Threatening b4, with a fork.

28...Be7. The bishop retreats, but now the e-pawn is pinned, enabling **29.Nd4!** The knights have tremendous power when they work together in the vicinity of an enemy king. At the moment, e6 is the threatened fork.

29...Rxc1; 30.Rxc1 Kh8. One fork eluded, but another one exists. **31.Nc6! Qc7; 32.Qxa6 Rc8; 33.Nf1.** White guards against back rank threats. Now the capture at e7 becomes a possibility. 33.Nxe7 Qxc1+; 34.Nf1 Rf8 keeps the game going for a while. **33...Rb8; 34.Nxe7!** From the other edge of the board, the White queen threatens mate with Qxf6!

34...Qxe7; 35.Rc8+ Rxc8; 36.Qxc8+.

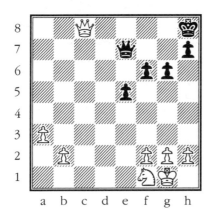

Alekhine resigned, a full piece down and missing a pawn as well.

14. MIKHAIL BOTVINNIK

Sixth World Champion (1948–1957, 1958–1960 and 1961–1963)

Botvinnik was the first world champion produced by the Soviet school of chess. The Communist party had selected chess as an intellectual battlefield in an ideological war. A rich chess culture allowed Botvinnik to acquire a vast arsenal of strategic and tactical weapons. He was so successful in the deployment of these weapons in tournaments games that he considered studying of his games the best method for achieving chess mastery.

Botvinnik's rigorous opening preparation led to sharp positions with a great deal of tactical activity. You can find almost any tactical motif in a collection of Botvinnik games, whether you are interested in the opening, middle game, or endgame. Our example game features plenty of action!

RAUZER VS. MIKHAIL BOTVINNIK
8th Soviet Championship, Leningrad, 1933
Sicilian Defense
1.e4 c5; 2.Nf3 Nc6; 3.d4 cxd4; 4.Nxd4 Nf6; 5.Nc3 d6; 6.Be2 g6. The game has transposed to the Classical Variation of the Sicilian Defense. Rauzer would become famous for a quite different approach to the Dragon, but one which is not possible with this move order. **7.Be3 Bg7; 8.Nb3 Be6; 9.f4 0–0.**

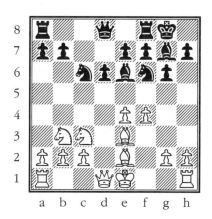

Botvinnik was no stranger to this variation throughout his career. **10.0–0.** 10.g4 d5; 11.f5! (11.e5 allows the intermezzo 11...d4! This was seen in a 1936 game between Levenfish and Botvinnik.) 11...Bc8; 12.exd5 Nb4; 13.d6! (13.fxg6 hxg6; 14.Bf3 Bxg4! The overworked White queen has to defend c2 and f3, more than one woman can bear. 15.Bxg4 Nxg4; 16.Qxg4 Nxc2+ wins material with a triple fork.) 13...Qxd6; 14.Bc5 Qf4; 15.Rf1 Qxh2; 16.Bxb4 Nxg4! Forcing a draw by perpetual check is the best Black can do. 17.Bxg4 Qg3+; 18.Rf2 Qg1+; 19.Rf1 Qg3+; 20.Rf2 Qg1+ with a draw in Alekhine vs. Botvinnik, from the strong international tournament at Nottingham, 1936 .

10...Na5; 11.Nxa5. The great Siegbert Tarrasch recommended 11.Nd4, while the swashbuckling Rudolf Spealmann suggested 11.f5, but in each case, Black can retreat with 11..Bd7.

11...Qxa5; 12.Bf3. White overprotects e4 and sets up a discovered attack with e5.

12...Bc4; 13.Re1.

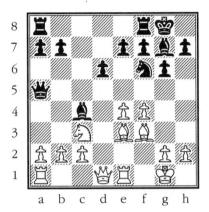

13...Rfd8! Botvinnik prepares the classical Sicilian break with ...d5. White has four pieces controlling that square, but the knight at c3 does not dare leave its post if the Dragon bishop at g7 awakens. **14.Qd2.** White may use an exchanging tactic typical of such positions, with Nd5 offering a trade of queens while also attacking f6 and e7, in each case with check. In addition, the d1 square is now cleared for the rook at a1.

14...Qc7. Botvinnik avoids the exchange of queens while keeping an eye on e5. This seems to diminish the control of d5, but there is a trick. **15.Rac1.** Botvinnik preferred 15.Qf2, but 15...Nd7 would have been a strong reply. **15...e5!?** The central counterattack begins. **16.b3.** 16.fxe5 dxe5; 17.Qf2 was given by Botvinnik, but Black can get some counterplay with 17...b5; 18.b3 b4!

16...d5!

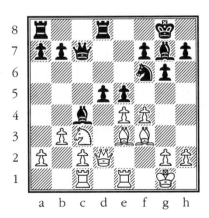

Both sides have a lot of firepower in the center. White thought that the attack on the bishop at c4 would result in a retreat. Instead, this intermezzo, threatening a fork after the pawn advances to d4, turns the tables.

17.exd5. Or, 17.bxc4 d4; 18.Nd5 with a counter-fork at f6 and c7. Then Black has 18...dxe3! This is stronger than an exchange of knights. (18...Nxd5; 19.cxd5 dxe3; 20.Rxe3. Taking with the queen returns to the main branch. 20...exf4; 21.Rb3 is a little better for White, but the bishops of opposite colors and weakness of White's dark squares give Black chances, too.)19.Qxe3 (19.Rxe3 Qxc4!? is promising for Black. There is a nasty pin on the d-file.) 19...Nxd5; 20.cxd5 exf4; 21.Qd3 is nothing special for White.

17...e4!

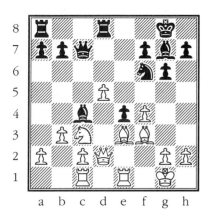

This was the move that Botvinnik planned, overlooked by Rauzer, **18.bxc4.** Tarrasch and other analysts explored the captures at e4, but neither worked out well. We have reason to believe they missed something.

18.Nxe4 Nxd5; 19.Kh1 at least gets the king off the dangerously exposed a7-b1 diagonal. (19.bxc4 Nxe3; 20.Qxe3?? Bd4 with a killer pin. 19.Qf2 Nxe3; 20.Rxe3 Be6 maintains the threat of ...Bd4.) 19...Nxe3; 20.Qxe3 Bd4; 21.Qd2 Bb2 uses a discovered attack to get at the rook on c1, but let's not forget that the bishop at c4 is hanging. Besides, the dark-squared bishop is the guardian of the holes on the kingside. 22.Qb4 (22.Qe3 invites a repetition with 22...Bd4.) 22...Bxc1.

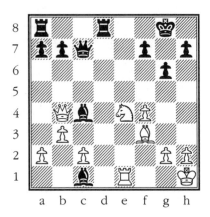

23.Nf6+! A fine intermezzo, exploiting the departure of the Dragon bishop. 23...Kh8; 24.Qc3! Ignoring the bishop, White sets up a discovered check threat which can easily lead to checkmate. Black has only one defense. 24...Bd2. Black forks White's remaining heavy artillery, and at the moment enjoys the advantage of an extra rook.

White simply maintains the pin. After all, the rook an a8 is not exactly doing anything of importance. 25.Qb2 Be6. The retreat of the bishop gives Black control of c3, so a discovered check is met by the interposition of a piece there. White's rook is still under attack, too. 26.Nd5+! Back the other way! The knight goes after the Black queen. 26...Bc3. The only reasonable try. 27.Nxc3. The knight has traveled from f6 to c3, but retains its power of discovered check, this time with the threat of Nb5+, winning the queen at c7. 27...Kg8 No more checks, but the knight races back to f6!; 28.Ne4 Qxf4; 29.Nf6+ Kf8.

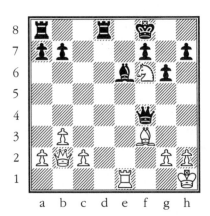

Botvinnik writes that White hasn't achieved anything here. Really? 30.Nd5! The threat is mate in one with Qh8. Black's queen is also attacked. He cannot capture with the bishop because that deflects it to d5, opening the e-file and enabling the same checkmating move. Black must capture with the rook. 30...Rxd5; 31.Qh8+ Ke7; 32.Qxa8. For the moment, material is even, but White is going to get one of the queenside pawns. For example 32...Qb4!?; 33.Ra1 Qc3; 34.Rg1 and the kingside is rock solid.

The Black rook must move and then pawns start to fall. Less worthy of analysis is 18.Bxe4 Nxe4; 19.Nxe4 Bxd5; 20.Qd3 Qc6; 21.Bf2 Re8. The knight is not pinned on the e-file, but the pin on the diagonal is critical. Botvinnik was right, there is nothing for White here. 22.Nd6 Rxe1+; 23.Rxe1 Bxg2; 24.Ne4! The interference on the diagonal forces Black to part with the bishop pair. 24...Bxe4; 25.Qxe4 Qxe4; 26.Rxe4 with a probable draw after Black guards the seventh rank with 26...Bf6.

The game followed a different path. **18...exf3; 19.c5 Qa5.**

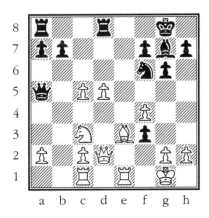

This is a critical position. White has an imposing pair of central pawns, but they are weak and require the attention of many of White's pieces. Because of the pin on the kngiht at c3, Black actually threatens to grab the pawn with the knight immediately. Rauzer remedied this by supporting the queen, but the Soviet analyst Grigoriyev, as a member of the jury considering this game for the brilliancy prize, found a better plan.

20.Red1? 20.Qd3 was the move that stood up for three decades before Botvinnik himself found 20...b6! White's pawn roller crumbles, no matter which pawn is captured 21.cxb6 axb6; 22.d6 fxg2; 23.Kxg2 Qa3 is fully playable for Black because White's extra pawn is meaningless given the weakness of every single White pawn. A simple demonstration of the danger is 24.Bxb6?? Rxd6 with a fork. 25.Bd4 (25.Qe3 Rxb6; 26.Qxb6 Qxc3 nets two pieces for the rook and the pawns are still weak.) 25...Nh5 Black has a discovered attack at d4 and a potential fork at f4. The alternative capture 21.gxf3 21...bxc5; 22.Rcd1 is nevertheless better than the line chosen in the game, because g4 is not available to the Black knight. Botvinnik's evaluation of the position as roughly level might be a bit optimistic.

20...Ng4!

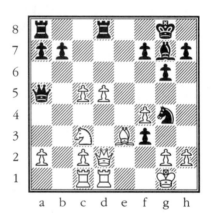

The discovered attack at c3 moves the knight into an excellent position, attacking the bishop and threatening to advance the f-pawn.

21.Bd4. 21.Ne4 leads to a long forcing variation resulting in a winning endgame for Black. 21...Qxd2; 22.Bxd2 Bd4+; 23.Kh1 fxg2+; 24.Kxg2 Rxd5; 25.h3 Nf6; 26.Nxf6+ Bxf6; 27.Be3 Rxd1; 28.Rxd1 Re8. White's pawns are simply too weak.

21...f2+. This is an exploitation of the overloaded bishop, which cannot cope with threats at c3 and f2 simultaneously.

22.Kf1. 22.Kh1 Rxd5 is utterly hopeless, as White's position is just a pin cushion. **22...Qa6+; 23.Qe2.** 23.Qd3 Bxd4!; 24.Qxa6 would not be bad if Black were obliged to capture at a6. There is an intermezzo, however. 24...Nxh2+!; 25.Ke2 f1Q+! The deflection takes the rook away from the bishop at d4. 26.Rxf1 bxa6. Black is up a piece.

23...Bxd4; 24.Rxd4.

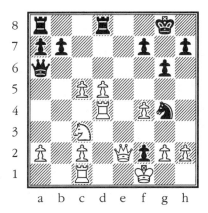

White is almost out of the woods. The pawns are still weak but in an endgame the king can safely march to c4. Capturing at h2 was probably what White expected, but Botvinnik played a stronger move.

24...Qf6!

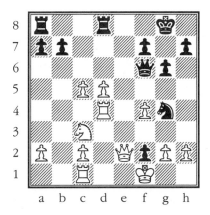

The rook and f-pawn are forked, and the queen can maneuver to h4.

25.Rcd1. 25.Qd3 Re8; 26.g3 (26.Re4? Rxe4; 27.Nxe4 Qxf4 would win quickly.) 26...Re3; 27.Qd2 Rae8 leads to a touchdown at e1. **25...Qh4; 26.Qd3 Re8.** There is no rush in going after the h-pawn. Botvinnik will take it when the time is right.

27.Re4 f5!; 28.Re6 Nxh2+!; 29.Ke2 Qxf4.

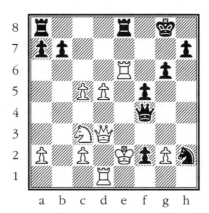

Rauzer had seen enough and resigned. The end would come in the form of 30.Rf1 Nxf1; 31.Kxf1 Rxe6; 32.dxe6 Qe5; 33.Kxf2 Qxc5+; 34.Kf1 Re8 with a hopeless position.

15. VASILY SMYSLOV

Seventh World Champion (1957–1958)

Smyslov lost his first challenge match against Botvinnik in 1954, but rebounded to wrest the title from him three years later. He is still a strong active Grandmaster who plays regularly in international competition. His talents outside of chess include operatic singing!

Known primarily as a positional player, Smyslov's best tactics usually arise in the late middlegame, after he has situated his forces on the best possible squares. This game was played during the Second World War, when there wasn't much chess activity. The Moscow Championship of 1943 was one of the strongest wartime tournaments, and it was quite a success for Smyslov, who defeated both Botvinnik and Alexander Kotov, one of the top Russian players and theoreticians at the time.

VASILY SMYSLOV VS. KOTOV
Moscow Championship, Soviet Union, 1943
Sicilian Defense: Closed Variation
1.e4 c5; 2.Nc3 Nc6; 3.g3 g6; 4.Bg2 Bg7; 5.d3 d6; 6.Nf3 e6; 7.Bg5 Nge7; 8.Qd2 h6; 9.Be3 e5; 10.0–0 Be6; 11.Ne1 Qd7.

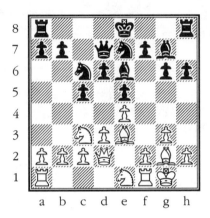

The opening has proceeded slowly, for a Sicilian Defense. Smyslov has a preference for the Closed Sicilian, which has a clear strategic contour and does not allow Black counterplay against the pawn at e4, which is thoroughly defended. White's next move is intended to prepare the advance of the b-pawn. Smyslov wants to resolve the queenside before undertaking kingside operations.

12.a3! Bh3. Black decides to get rid of the light-squared bishops. This only makes sense in the context of a kingside attack, but as we shall see, it is White who has aspirations on that flank. **13.f4 Nd4; 14.Rb1 exf4; 15.Bxf4 Bxg2; 16.Qxg2 0–0.**

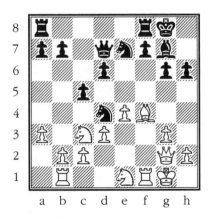

The game has opened up a bit, and that sets the stage for tactical operations, which are hard to carry out in closed positions. The f-file, a8-h1 diagonal and c1–h6 diagonal are potential staging areas.

17.g4. The point of this move is not a kingside pawnstorm, but rather greater control of f5. The presence of the queen on the g-file, where the Black monarch resides, gives rise to tactical possibilities involving pins and discovered checks, once the g-pawn moves out of the way. White already thinks in terms of placing a knight at f5.

17...Rad8; 18.Kh1 Ne6. Black has marshaled all of his forces in defense of the kingside. This makes Smyslov's task very difficult. On the one hand, he needn't worry about queenside counterplay, for the moment. On the other hand, how to get past all those defenders? **19.Bd2 d5.** The standard Sicilian break in the center gives Black a roughly equal game.

20.Nf3.

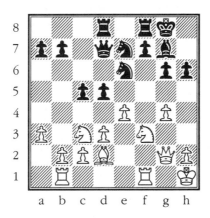

Black should reduce White's attacking options by capturing at e4. If White recaptures with the knight, then control of f5 is lessened. Taking with the pawn leaves e4 weak and opens the d-file, which presently belongs to Black.

20...d4?; 21.Ne2 Nc6; 22.Qh3 Kh7; 23.Ng3 f6. Preventing both threats, 24.g5 and 24.Bxh6 Bxh6; 25.g5, but weakening the Kingside. Instead the quiet 23...Qc7 seems acceptable.

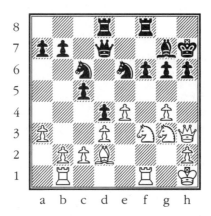

24.Nf5! This is a positional sacrifice, which gives rise to many tactical possibilities. Black can't refuse the offer, because the pawn at h6 is under assault.

24...gxf5. 24...g5 gives Black a permanently terrible bishop and White can play slowly, doubling rooks on the f-file, before launching a major attack. **25.gxf5 Nc7; 26.Rg1 Ne8.** 26...Rh8; 27.Bxh6! Bxh6 (27...Kg8; 28.Rxg7+ Qxg7; 29.Rg1) 28.Rg6! Qg7; 29.Rxg7 Kxg7; 30.Qg3+ (the decisive double threat) and 31.Qxc7 26...b5; 27.Rxg7+!! removes the crucial defender at g7. 27...Qxg7 (27...Kxg7; 28.Rg1+ Kf7; 29.Qh5+ Ke7; 30.Rg7+ wins.) 28.Rg1 drives the queen away from the h-pawn, and White wins.

27.Rg6. The rook moves into a triple attack, targeting two pawns and the bishop. The pressure at f6 is not significant now, because the f-pawn is well defended, but can become a factor later in some circumstances. White is also ready to double rooks on the only open file.

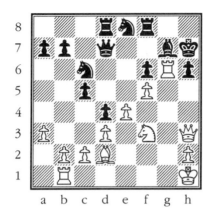

27...Rf7; 28.Rbg1 Kg8. One pin is broken, but now the bishop cannot move. White can capture the h-pawn with three different pieces. **29.Rxh6.** There is a mating threat at h8, thanks to the pin on the bishop.

29...Kf8. The king tries to flee to the queenside. If this can be accomplished, Black will be able to mount a counterattack on the h-file. The king must be confined to the center. **30.Rh7 Ke7.** 30...Ne5 follows the advice that one should exchange a piece which is not involved in defense for an attacker or potential attacker. 31.Nxe5 fxe5; 32.Bh6 is, however, impossible to meet. 32...Bxh6; 33.Qxh6+ Ke7. If Black simply interposes a piece then f6 wins. 34.Rxf7+ Kxf7; 35.Qh7+ and mate in two.

31.Qh5! Kd6.

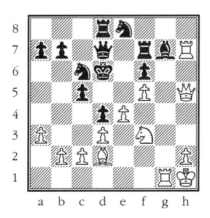

31...Rc8 makes room for the king, but Smyslov was prepared with 32.Ng5! The decoy removes an important defender of the king. 32...fxg5; 33.Bxg5+ and now the king can run or the knight can be interposed.

The first plan leads to 33...Kd6; 34.Bf4+ Ke7; 35.f6+! The pawn can be captured by four different Black pieces, but each capture loses. 35...Kxf6 (35...Bxf6; 36.Qxf7+ Kd8; 37.Qxd7#). 35...Rxf6; 36.Rgxg7+ Nxg7; 37.Rxg7+ wins. 35...Nxf6; 36.Rgxg7! Nxh5; 37.Rxf7+ Ke6; 38.Rxd7 where the fork 38...Nf6 is mated by 39.Rd6#) 36.Rg6+ Ke7; 37.Bg5+ Nf6; 38.Rxf6! Rxf6; 39.Rxg7+ etc.

The other plan doesn't work out any better. 33...Nf6; 34.Rxg7! A deflection, because the rook is drawn away from the knight, and a decoy, because at g7 the rook will be more vulnerable. 34...Rxg7; 35.Bxf6+ Kxf6; 36.Qh6+ is a fork which wins the rook and more. **32.Bf4+.**

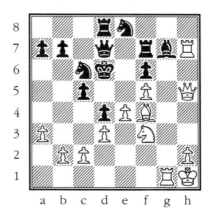

32...Ne5. The block provides only temporary safety, because White can still open up the position. 32...Ke7 loses to 33.Ng5! fxg5; 34.Bxg5+ Kd6; 35.Bf4+ Ke7; 36.f6+ as in the previous note.

33.Bxe5+ fxe5; 34.f6!

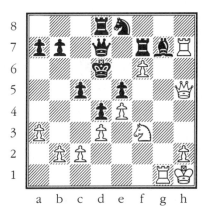

Smyslov himself noted the importance of pinning and interference themes which come together to make this the decisive blow in the game.

34...Nxf6. The knight interferes with the defense of e5. 34...Bxf6 drops the rook to 35.Rxf7. 34...Rxf6; 35.Rgxg7 Nxg7; 36.Qxe5+ Kc6; 37.Qxf6+ Kb5; 38.Rxg7 is a simple win.

35.Qxe5+ Kc6.

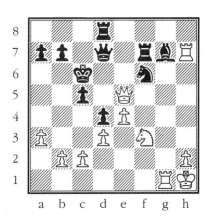

White is still down a piece for two pawns, but the rook is overloaded at f7, having to defend both g7 and f6.

36.Rhxg7! Kb5. The pawn at d4 has three defenders, but they are all out of commission. The pawn at c5 is pinned, the queen at d7 must protect the rook at f7, and Black's other rook can't do anything.

37.Nxd4+! Kb6. 37...Qxd4; 38.Qxd4 cxd4; 39.Rxf7 37...Qxd4; 38.Qxd4 cxd4; 39.Rxf7 is hopeless for Black. **38.b4!**

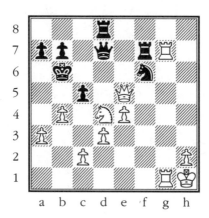

The threat of checkmate with Qxc5 and Qa5 effectively ends the game.

38...Rc8; 39.Rxf7 Qxf7; 40.Qd6+! Rc6; 41.Nxc6 Nxe4; 42.bxc5+. Black resigned.

16. MIKHAIL TAL

Eighth World Champion (1960-1961)

Tal, the magician from Riga, is the champion best known for his sacrificial attacks. Affectionately known as Mischa, Tal was admired and loved by his competitors as well as his millions of fans. He raised the part of attack to new levels, relying on instinct as well as calculation to boldly invest material in order to gain access to the enemy fortress.

To accomplish his sacrificial goals, Tal relied on the use of all of his tactical ability. His deep insights into the possibilities for simple tactics enables him to construct combinations which ranked among the most beautiful ever played. His brief reign as world champion was the highlight of his career but he distinguished himself in tournaments play as well.

BORIS SPASSKY VS. MIKHAIL TAL
International Tournament, Tallin 1973
Nimzo-Indian Defense

Two former World Champions meet in an important tournament contest. Spassky takes up one of his favorite weapons, the Leningrad Varation, against Tal's Nimzo-Indian. Spassky is one of the Leningraders who gave the variation its reputation. Tal was well prepared. The middlegame tactics come fast and furious, and Tal's magical abilities carry the day.

1.d4 Nf6; 2.c4 e6; 3.Nc3 Bb4; 4.Bg5 h6; 5.Bh4 c5; 6.d5 b5!?

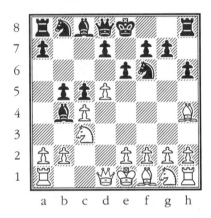

A gambit in the style of the then popular Benko Gambit. From a tactical standpoint, it must be noted that the key to the position is a pair of pins!

7.dxe6. The challenge is accepted. **7...fxe6; 8.cxb5 d5.** Black has a mobile pawn center. The threat is 9...d4, exploiting the pin. 8...Qa5 adds pressure to the pin but allows the devastation of the kingside pawn barrier with 9.Bxf6 gxf6. After 10.Qc2 Kf7; 11.e3 a6; 12.Bd3 Bb7; 13.Nge2! White eventually won in Spassky vs. Posner, Canada 1971.

9.e3 0-0; 10.Nf3?! An obvious move but a poor one. Tal noted that 10.Bd3 d4; 11.exd4 cxd4; 12.a3 was better for White, though a draw was the eventual conclusion in Spassky vs. Unzicker, from the European Team Championship of the same year.

10...Qa5. 10...Nbd7; 11.Bd3 e5; 12.Bf5 e4 is far too ambitious and Spassky himself refuted it. 13.Be6+ forks g8 and d5. 13...Kh8; 14.Bxd5 Nxd5; 15.Bxd8 Nxc3; 16.bxc3 Bxc3+; 17.Nd2 Rxd8 didn't bring enough for the queen. 18.Rc1 Ba5; 19.0-0 Ne5; 20.Qh5 Bxd2; 21.Qxe5 Bxc1; 22.Rxc1 Bb7; 23.h4. Black resigned. Spassky vs. Liebert, Sochi 1967.

11.Bxf6! There is no longer a pin, and Black must act before the knight gets to e4. **11...Rxf6; 12.Qd2.** The queen should have stayed on the first rank, protecting the rook and enabling the advance of the a-pawn to a3. By walking into a pin, Tal is given tactical opportunities. 12...a6! Opening new lines. **13.bxa6.** 13.b6 was better, keeping the a-file closed and, if Black captures the pawn, reducing the power of the pin on the knight at c3.

13...Nc6; 14.Be2.

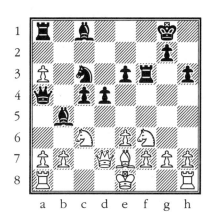

Now the fireworks begin.

14...d4!! A fantastic conception, typical of Tal. He plans to sacrifice an exchange on the next move. The power of the pin on the knight at c3 is so great that material investment is a minor concern. **15.exd4 Rxf3!** Black removes the defender of the pawn at d4. **16.Bxf3.** Ah, but the bishop at f3 now pins the knight at c6, which is under attack. Tal pays the frightened steed no heed and continues the attack.

16...cxd4.

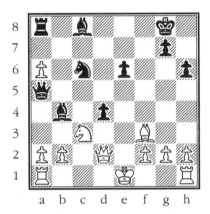

17.0–0. 17.Bxc6 fails to dxc3 with nasty business on the a5-e1 diagonal. White must get the king off that line.

17...dxc3; 18.bxc3 Bxc3. The fork of the queen and the rook at a1 is just part of the story. Black has three minor pieces, all of which can be used to create threats. The White rooks sit passively. **19.Qd6.** Spassky relied on this to save the rook at a1. Tal had seen more deeply into the position.

19...Rxa6. 19...Bxa1; 20.Qxc6 wins material. **20.Bxc6.**

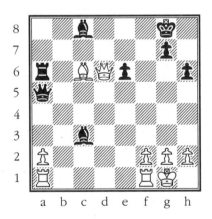

20...Bb4! The bishop retreats to remove the defender of the White bishop, which is pinned. Tal wins two pieces for a rook, but White gets a little counterplay so he has to be careful.

21.Qb8! Rxc6; 22.Rac1. The x-ray along the c-file can,

fortunately, be blocked. **22...Bc5; 23.Rc2.** The threat of doubling rooks looks very dangerous **23...Qa4!**

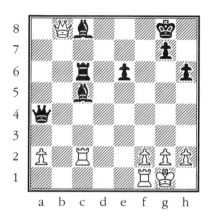

Cataloging the pins and threats in this position might take a while! White could double rooks, but that walks into a bishop sacrifice and a crushing discovered attack.

24.Qb3. White didn't have much choice but to defend the rook, 24.Rfc1? loses instantly to 24...Bxf2+! Black wins one of the rooks. 24.Rd2 threatens a back rank check which forks king and bishop, but Black blocks with 24...Bd4 and can support the bishop with ...e5.

24...Qf4! Tal was certainly not going to exchange queens, but which square should the queen go to? 24...Qe4; 25.Rfc1 Bb7 leads to another tactical flurry. 26.Qxb7 Bxf2+!; 27.Kf1 (27.Kxf2 Rxc2+; 28.Rxc2 Qxb7 ; 27.Kh1 loses spectacularly to 27...Rxc2!!; 28.Qxe4 Rxc1+ and mates.) 27...Qd3+; 28.Kxf2 Rxc2+; 29.Rxc2 Qxc2+; 30.Kg3 Qxa2 gives Black an extra pawn. Tal saw all this, but was not convinced that the endgame is winnable. Indeed, it is unlikely that White would have any serious losing chances.

25.Qg3. Another attempt to get queens off the board. 25.Qf3!? might have been considered, though Black is clearly better after 25...Qc7; 26.Rfc1 Bb7; 27.h3 Qb6 where the bishops will be very powerful. **25...Qf5!** The only move, keeping control of c5 and f2 which are flashpoints for tactics.

26.Rfc1. More pressure on the c-file. Tal's queen has done a remarkable job of attacking and defending, using just the right squares. Still, the rest of the pieces must be made more comfortable.

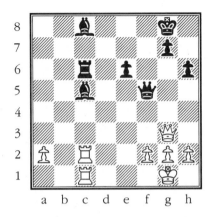

26...Bb7. This not only defends c6, but sets up later threats on the long diagonal. **27.Qf3.** White dearly wants to exchange queens, but that is simply out of the question. 27.Qb8+ forks the king and bishop and seems to win a piece, but after 27...Kh7; 28.Qxb7 a rude awakening comes via 28...Bxf2+!; 29.Kf1 (29.Rxf2 Rxc1+; 30.Rf1 Rxf1#) 29...Rxc2; 30.Rxc2 Qxc2 and it is Black who emerges with the extra piece.

27...Qg5; 28.Qb3. 28.Qg3? meets a familiar fate: 28...Bxf2+!; 29.Qxf2 (29.Kxf2 Rxc2+; 30.Rxc2 Qf5+) 29...Qxc1+! Black wins a rook or gets into a totally lost endgame. **28...Rc7!** The bishop on b7 turns into a monster, supporting a mate threat at g2. **29.g3.**

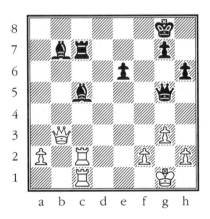

29.Qxe6+ Rf7; 30.g3 Bxf2+! is deadly, because the rook at c2 must stay put to defend its colleague at c1.

29...Bxf2+! At long last, the key move actually appears on the board! **30.Kxf2 Qf6+.** A bit of sloppiness. 30...Qf5+ was better, because the queen could maneuver to e4 and end the game more quickly. Still, the win is clear.

31.Ke1 Qe5+; 32.Kf1 Ba6+; 33.Kg1 Qd4+; 34.Kg2 Qe4+. Finally the queen crawls to the right square.

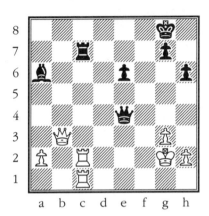

35.Kg1. 35.Kh3 Rxc2; 36.Qxc2 Bf1+; 37.Rxf1 Qxc2 is not worth contesting. **35...Bb7.** The naked White king is defenseless on the diagonal. The rook at c2 can't move off the rank without allowing mate at g2.

36.h4 Qh1+; 37.Kf2 Rf7+; 38.Ke2 Qe4+.

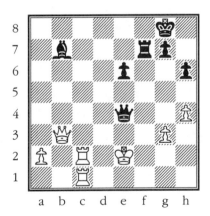

Spassky resigned. He could have continued to time control with 39.Qe3 Ba6+; 40.Kd2 Rd7+ but it was hardly worth the bother.

17. TIGRAN PETROSIAN

Ninth World Champion (1963–1969)

Of all the World Champions, Tigran Petrosian is perhaps the last name that comes to mind when tactics are the topic of discussion. The Georgian tiger was a slow developer, not learning the game until the age of twelve and making master only at the age of 18. He developed a unique style, patiently and cunningly awaiting enemy mistakes, especially when the opponent overextended his position.

Petrosian loved positional chess, and Capablanca's games were an important part of his study. The hypermodern spirit of Nimzowitsch also infused his play with positional considerations and even his choice of openings. The semi-closed positions of the Caro-Kann and French Defenses did not lead to the swashbuckling attacks seen in the more popular Sicilian Defense. Tactics were employed only when necessary. His ability to calculate was second to none, but the logic of the position, not romantic or flashy tendencies, guided his play.

Living up to his nickname, the Tiger, Petrosian is remembered more for cunning than for brilliance, but his tactics, when revealed, were impressive. This important contest against Taimanov is typical of the effectiveness of Petrosian's tactical play.

TIGRAN PETROSIAN VS. TAIMANOV
22nd Soviet Championship, Moscow, 1955
Semi-Slav Defense
1.d4 Nf6; 2.c4 e6; 3.Nf3 d5; 4.Nc3 c6; 5.e3 Nbd7; 6.Bd3 Bb4!?; 7.0–0 0–0; 8.Qc2.

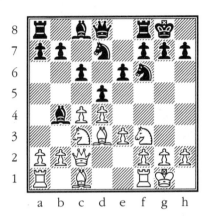

Taimanov changes his mind and retreats his bishop. If he wants the bishop on d6, he should capture at c4 first, before White has a chance to protect the pawn with b3.

8...Bd6? 8...dxc4 is considered stronger. 9.Bxc4 Bd6 and Black is ready for ...e5; **9.b3! dxc4.** 9...e5?! is no longer playable; 10.cxd5 cxd5; 11.Nb5! **10.bxc4 e5; 11.Bb2 Re8; 12.Ne4!**

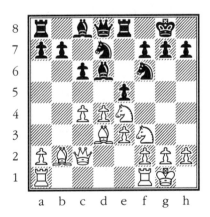

White blocks the advance of Black's e-pawn, and forces the exchange of knights which reduces Black's defensive capability.

12...Nxe4; 13.Bxe4 h6. Petrosian thought that 13...g6 was the lesser of the evils, but 14.Bd3! (14.Rad1 Qe7; 15.Rfe1 f5; 16.dxe5 Bb4 was unclear, according to Petrosian.) 14...Qe7; 15.c5! Bc7; 16.Bc4 was proposed as an improvement by Novotelnov. The pin on the f-pawn is annoying. For example, Black cannot play ...h6 because of Qxg6+! 13...g6?; 14.Bd3! Qe7; 15.c5 Bc7; 16.Bc4! Novotelnov. **14.Rad1 exd4; 15.Bh7+!** The intermezzo is the key to White's plan. The bishop gets away from e4. 15.Rxd4 would have allowed Black to attack the bishop and defend h7 in one stroke with 15...Nf6!

15...Kh8; 16.Rxd4.

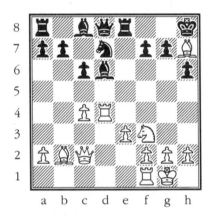

This is an extended rook lift. The rook will operate along the fourth rank, rather than the third. Black usually can control squares on the fourth rank easily, so this tactic is much rarer than the normal rook lift.

16...Bc5. Petrosian liked 16...Be7 but 17.Ne5 Rf8; 18.Nxd7! Bxd7; 19.Rfd1 applies a crushing pin that wins a piece. 16...Qe7 avoids pins, yet also fails to satisfy after 17.Re4 Qf8; 18.Rh4, threatening to exploit the pin on the g-pawn with Rxh6. 18...Ne5.

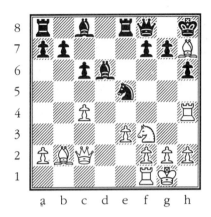

This interferes with the diagonal, but there is a hidden pin on the h-file. There are three plans to consider, and each is ripe with tactical possibilities.

White might exchange pieces in the center with 19.Nxe5 Bxe5; 20.Bxe5 Rxe5; 21.Qb2, attacking the rook at e5, and now 21...Qe7; 22.Bb1! sets up a threat of Qc2, with strong pressure on the kingside. 22...f6; 23.Rd1 prepares to use a deflection check at d8, if necessary, but 23...Be6; 24.Qc2 f5 is about even.

19.Ng5? is given by Ken Smith, but he only considers capturing the knight and the advance of the f-pawn. There is a third line which is far more complicated. 19...hxg5? invites mate in two. 20.Bg8+ is a discovered check that will be followed by mate at h7. One logical defense is 19...f5, which is met by 20.Bg6! The knight is pinned, remember!

20...Re7 (20...Nxg6; 21.Rxh6+ Kg8; 22.Rxg6 Be5; 23.c5 Bxb2; 24.Qc4+! The threat of Qh4 is overwhelming.) 21.c5! Bc7; 22.Bxe5! Bxe5; 23.Qc4! Black has only one defense to the threatened check at f7. 23...Be6 avoids immediate disaster, but 24.Nxe6 Qf6; 25.Nxg7! Qxg6; 26.Nh5 retains White's material advantage. The most interesting reply is 19...Qe7!? Black uses a counter-pin against the White pieces on the kingside; 20.f4 is the threat which Smith pointed out, but the weakness at e3 is too great. 20...Ng4 (20...Bc5 unleashes a fury of tactics. 21.Bxe5 Bxe3+; 22.Kh1 f6 gets terminated by 23.Bg8!!

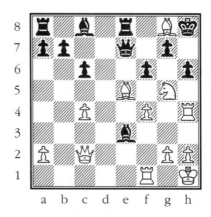

Black can only defend h7 with 23...f5 but then the pin on all three kingside pawns proves fatal after 24.Bf7!) 21.Be4 f6 and White no longer has any real compensation for the piece.

The last option, 19.Nd4!?, prevents Black from guarding the kingside with ...f5 and therefore deserves consideration. 19...Nxc4 exploits the overworked queen, which needs to guard c4 and h7. (19...g6; 20.Bxg6 fxg6; 21.f4 drives away the defender of g6, and the kingside falls quickly. 19...Qe7; 20.Re4 sets a strong pin. 20...g6 traps the bishop, but the price is too high. 21.Bxg6 fxg6; 22.f4 turns the game in White's favor.) 20.Nf5 Bxf5; 21.Rxh6 Nxb2; 22.Rh5 keeps the attack going. Even though the bishop at f5 attacks two White pieces, neither can be safely captured. 22...g6; 23.Bxg6+ Kg7; 24.Bxf5 gives White considerable compensation for the piece because the knight at b2 is trapped. 24...Be5; 25.Bd7! White opens up the path to h7, while attacking the rook at e8, and should win.

In any case, Black decided to play the bishop to c5.

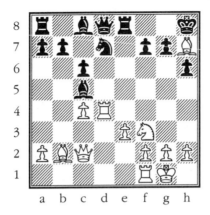

17.Rf4! The rook finds new employment at f4, attacking f7 and protecting c4. **17...Qe7.** Black was not about to allow White to pin with Rd1. **18.Re4!**

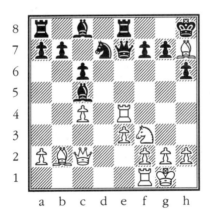

Another shift, creating a self-interference on the diagonal. The queen is driven back to the first rank, which makes h4 a safe square for the rook.

18...Qf8; 19.Rh4! The attacking formation we saw in the notes to Black's 16th move comes into play. The difference is that the Black bishop is at c5 here. This makes the defense far more difficult.

The immediate threat is Rxh6, and Black cannot block with 19...Nf6 because that does not prevent White from playing 20.Rxh6, as 20...gxh6 allows 21.Bxf6#.

19...f6. A diagonal is blocked, but a hole is created. **20.Bg6 Re7; 21.Rh5!** The rook steps out of the way, so that the knight can get to h4. Black cannot use the knight at d7 in defense now because the bishop at c5 would hang.

21...Bd6; 22.Rd1! Though we are well past the opening, the rook finally manages to develop with tempo, on the square it was destined to occupy. **22...Be5.**

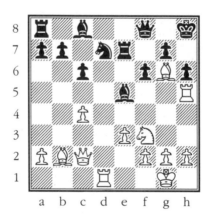

Black finally controls e5, but there is a different pin in the air.

23.Ba3! c5. The pin is blocked, but the attack continues on the kingside.

24.Nh4!

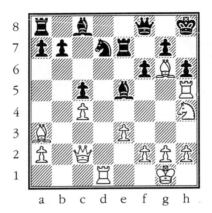

Black resigned, with good reason. 24...Qg8; 24...Qd8; 25.Bxc5 Re6; 26.Bf7 wins the rook and more, for example 26...Ra6; 27.Ng6+ Kh7; 28.Nf8+ Kh8; 29.Qh7#; 25.Bh7! Deflection. 25...Qxh7; 26.Ng6+. A fork, which picks up the whole rook, and more. 26...Kg8; 27.Nxe7+ Kh8; 28.Qxh7+ Kxh7; 29.Nxc8 Rxc8; 30.Rxd7 with an extra rook for White.

18. BORIS SPASSKY

Tenth World Champion (1969–1972)

Boris Spassky brought a totally different style of chess to his matches. Spassky loved wide open positions, was happy to contest main line openings, and rarely let an opportunity for a tactical brawl slip through his fingers. From his early days he was uncorking spectacular combinations at the board, and even used gambit openings to set up exciting possibilities.

All this lasted only until his defeat at the hands of Bobby Fischer, a psychologically devastating blow which reduced his ambitions in the chess world and led to a more cautious style which results in many draws. His games in the post-Fischer era just don't have the same sparkle as his early efforts. This game against the great David Bronstein is one of Spassky's best, a sparkling contest which received a special prize as the best game played in the 1960 Soviet Championship. Spassky uses the old-fashioned King's Gambit, which had rarely been used by World Champions.

BORIS SPASSKY VS. BRONSTEIN
Soviet Championship, Leningrad, 1960
King's Gambit Accepted

1.e4 e5; 2.f4 exf4; 3.Nf3 d5; 4.exd5 Bd6; 5.Nc3 Ne7; 6.d4 0-0; 7.Bd3 Nd7; 8.0-0 h6; 9.Ne4 Nxd5; 10.c4 Ne3; 11.Bxe3 fxe3; 12.c5 Be7; 13.Bc2 Re8; 14.Qd3.

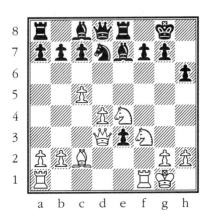

14...e2? 14...Nf8 was necessary. Spassky wastes no time worrying about his rook. As long as one rook winds up on the f-file, it will be enough.

15.Nd6!? 15.Rf2 is good enough, but Spassky wanted to win with style. **15...Nf8?** Too late! 15...Bxd6 was correct. The e-pawn is defended by the rook, and the Black king has a crawl space. 16.Qh7+ Kf8; 17.cxd6 exf1Q+; 18.Rxf1 cxd6; 19.Qh8+ Ke7; 20.Re1+ can be met by 20...Ne5! because the White queen is under attack. 21.Qxg7 Rg8; 22.Qxh6 eats a few pawns but Black can pin the d-pawn with 22...Qb6. The pin can be re-established with 23.Kh1 and White is a bit better after either 23...Qxb2; 24.dxe5 Qxc2; 25.exd6+ Kd7; 26.Ne5+ Ke8 (26...Kd8; 27.Qf6+ Ke8; 28.Qe7#) 27.Nxf7+! Kd7 (27...Kxf7; 28.Re7#) 28.Ne5+ Ke8; 29.d7+! Bxd7; 30.Nc6+! and mate follows, or 23...Be6; 24.dxe5 d5 where the extra pawn and vulnerable Black king provide compensation for the exchange.

16.Nxf7. Destroying the barrier is worth more than a rook! **16...exf1Q+; 17.Rxf1.**

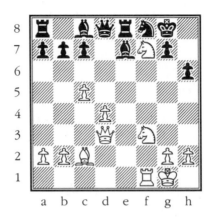

Now the fun really begins.

17...Bf5. 17...Kxf7; 18.Ne5+ Kg8 leads to an elegant finish. 19.Qh7+!! Nxh7; 20.Bb3+ Qd5; 21.Bxd5+ Be6; 22.Bxe6+ Kh8; 23.Ng6#. 17...Qd5 walks into shish-kabob after 18.Bb3 when 18...Qxf7; 19.Bxf7+ Kxf7; 20.Qc4+ Kg6; 21.Qg8 chokes the back alleys. Black cannot survive, for example, 21...Bf6; 22.Nh4+! Bxh4; 23.Qf7+ Kh7; 24.Qxe8 Ng6; 25.Rf7 with Black's three uncoordinated pieces proving no match for White's big guns.

18.Qxf5. White has achieved material balance but the devastation of the kingside is just beginning. **18...Qd7.** 18...Qc8 can be met by a number of moves. Each contains interesting tactics. 19.Qd3 (19.Bb3 sets up 19...Qxf5; 20.Nxh6+. The double check recovers the queen with a material advantage for White. 20...Kh7; 21.Nxf5 Bf6; 22.g4 gives White two pawns and a continuing attack for the exchange. 19.Qf4 is more or less the same as the game.) 19...Bf6 (19...Kxf7; 20.Ne5+ Kg8; 21.Qh7+Nxh7; 22.Bb3+ Kh8; 23.Ng6# is the mate we saw earlier.) 20.N3e5 Bxe5; 21.Nxe5 c6; 22.Bb3+ Ne6 (22...Kh8 is mated quickly. 23.Rxf8+ Rxf8; 24.Ng6+ Kh7; 25.Nxf8+ Kh8; 26.Qh7#) 23.Qg6 Re7 loses to the lovely 24.Rf7! Rxf7; 25.Bxe6 Qf8; 26.Bxf7+ Kh8; 27.Qf5 and the knight gets to g6 unless Black gives up the queen at f7.

19.Qf4 Bf6; 20.N3e5.

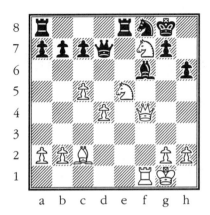

20...Qe7. 20...Bxe5; 21.Nxe5 Qe7; 22.Bb3+ Ne6 (22...Kh8; 23.Qg4 prepares Rf7.) 23.Ng6 Qd7; 24.Qe4 wins at least a piece, because Nf4 will bring enough force to bear at e6. Black can set up an attack on the pawn at d4 but it is not enough. 24...Rad8; 25.Rf8+!! Rxf8; 26.Bxe6+ etc.

21.Bb3. The rest is forced. **21...Bxe5; 22.Nxe5+ Kh7; 23.Qe4+.** Black resigned. 23...g6 gets demolished by 24.Rxf8! Rxf8; 25.Qxg6+ Kh8; 26.Qxh6+ Qh7; 27.Ng6#.

19. ROBERT FISCHER

Eleventh World Champion (1972–1975)

The enigmatic Bobby Fischer remains the most recognizable chess name, even though he has only played a few games since his abdication of the World Championship title in the mid-1970s. Fischer is a larger-than-life figure whose chessplaying is certainly among the best of all time. His thorough command of all phases of the game enabled him to sweep aside almost all opposition.

Fischer has campaigned for changing the rules of chess to de-emphasize the domination of opening theory, letting more games be decided in the middlegame and endgame. His mastery of fundamental tactics makes him almost unbeatable in those phases of the game. Unfortunately, Fischer's continued self-imposed exile from the chess world leaves us without new examples, but his legacy of over 1000 recorded games is sufficient to find many instances of his tactical prowess.

Bobby Fischer's tactical skill has never been questioned. From the opening to the endgame he finds countless ways to make his opponents feel uncomfortable. He could find deep secrets in the opening. We have selected one of his less familiar games, but one which shows his mastery of tactics throughout. In a very standard opening, Fischer finds a resource that had eluded co-author Shamkovich just two years earlier. Fischer's improvement is so powerful that it obliterated the popular variation in the opening!

BOBBY FISCHER VS. STEINMEYER
United States Championship, New York, 1963
Caro-Kann Defense
1.e4 c6; 2.d4 d5; 3.Nc3 dxe4; 4.Nxe4 Bf5; 5.Ng3 Bg6; 6.Nf3 Nf6; 7.h4 h6; 8.Bd3 Bxd3; 9.Qxd3 e6; 10.Bd2.

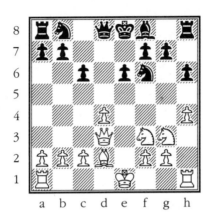

The quiet Classical Variation of the Caro-Kann is the last place you might expect to see tactical fireworks, but in Fischer's hands, any opening could turn ugly at a moment's notice!

10...Nbd7. 10...Qc7!?; 11.c4 Nbd7; 12.Bc3 would have transposed to Fischer-Donner, Varna Olympiad 1962, a game with which Black was no doubt familiar, but Fischer got a very good position there and Steinmeyer had a specific variation in mind.

11.0–0–0 Qc7; 12.c4 0–0–0. 12...Bd6 was preferred by Fischer, who gave further: 13.Ne4 (13.Ne2 0–0–0; 14.Kb1 c5=) 13...Bf4! The removal of the dark squared bishops solves Black's opening problems. **13.Bc3!**

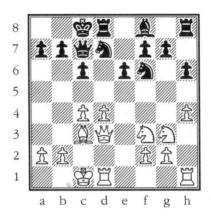

We are entering the middlegame now. White has a tiny edge in development and control of the center. Black has a weakness at f7, but there doesn't seem to be any way to exploit it. Steinmeyer was no doubt familiar with a game played in the Soviet Union in 1961, and was looking forward to a comfortable game.

13...Qf4+? 13...Bd6! is the correct move, overprotecting e5 and preventing the incursion of the knight. 14.Ne4 Bf4+; 15.Kb1 Ne5! exploits the pin on the d-file to gain equality. 16.Nxe5 Bxe5 is playable because of the pin on the d-pawn.

14.Kb1 Nc5? Black can't resist testing the pin, but the move backfires once the White queen moves away, creating a threat at c5. 14...Qc7 was best, admitting that the check was a mistake. Black loses a tempo, but that's all. 15.Ne4 Nxe4; 16.Qxe4 Nf6; 17.Qe2 is just a little better for White, but now Black can play 17...Qf4 contesting the e4-square. **15.Qc2 Nce4.**

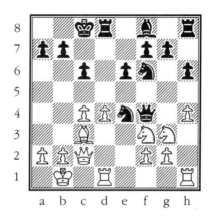

This position had already been reached in Shamkovich-Goldberg, from the 1961 Moscow Championship, where White continued ineffectively. 15...Ncd7 meets a similar fate to that of the game: 16.Ne5! Nxe5; 17.dxe5 Nd7 (17...Ng4; 18.Rxd8+ Kxd8; 19.Rd1+ Kc8; 20.Rd4 x-rays the queen and knight.) 18.Rd4 Qxe5; 19.Rxd7! as analyzed by Fischer himself. When the queen, under attack from the bishop at c3, retreats, the rook at d8 falls with check and White has gained a piece for a pawn.

16.Ne5! 16.Ba5 was played in the above-mentioned game, and Steinmeyer no doubt was quite pleased with the prospect of meeting that variation. But Fischer's improvement destroys the entire variation with the queen check at f4. For the record, Shamkovich regained the advantage after 16...b6; 17.Nxe4 Nxe4; 18.Rhe1 when his opponent went wrong with 18...f5?!; 19.Ne5 Bd6; 20.Ng6! Qxf2; 21.Re2 Qg3; 22.Nxh8 Rxh8; 23.Be1 then broke through after 23...Qg4; 24.c5 bxc5; 25.Qc4 Kb7; 26.Rd3 Bc7; 27.Rc2 Nd6; 28.Qxc5 Qe4; 29.Re3 Qd5; 30.Rxe6 Qxc5; 31.dxc5 and went on to win the game.

Black could have done better with 18...Nxf2; 19.Qxf2 (19.Bxb6 Nxd1; 20.Bxd8 Ne3; 21.Rxe3 Qxe3; 22.Ba5 Bd6; 23.c5 Bc7; 24.Bd2 Qe2 is better for Black) 19...bxa5; 20.d5 Bb4; 21.Qxa7 Bxe1; 22.Qa8+ Qb8; 23.Qxc6+ Qc7; 24.Rxe1 Qxc6; 25.dxc6 Kc7; 26.b3 Rhf8; 27.Re5 a4! in a very complicated endgame.

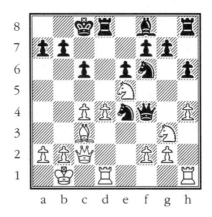

16...Nxf2. 16...Nxg3 doesn't work. Fischer demonstrated the following lines: 17.fxg3 Qxg3; 18.Rd3 Qf4; 19.Rf3 Qe4; 20.Nxf7 when White wins material. 16...Nxc3+; 17.bxc3! Rg8 (17...Ng4; 18.Nh5! Qf5; 19.Qxf5 exf5; 20.Nxf7) 18.Rd3 h5; 19.Rf3 Qh6; 20.Nxf7 and the fork is even worse. 16...Rg8 is countered by the clever retreat 17.Be1! Nxg3.

17.Rdf1!

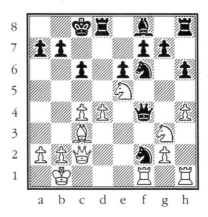

Black resigned, because of 17...Qxg3; 18.Rxf2 The threat is Rh3 or Rf3, trapping the queen. 18...Qe3; 19.Re2 Qf4; 20.Nxf7 and the fork wins.

20. ANATOLY KARPOV

Twelfth World Champion (1975-1985, FIDE 1993-present)

Anatoly Karpov has a very quiet and methodical style, and tactical brawls are very rare in his games as an adult. He has inherited the World Championship title twice, first when Bobby Fischer refused to defend it, and almost twenty years later when Garry Kasparov bolted FIDE and set up his own organization. He defeated Victor Korchnoi three straight times, but when faced with the challenge of Kasparov he was not up to the task and has never defeated him in a match. From time to time he shows flashes of the dominating skill he showed in the 1970s and early 1980s, and remains a formidable opponent.

Karpov's wins are mostly technical. He accumulates small advantages and reaches winning positions with ease. Tactics in his games are mostly buried, as Karpov is able to anticipate enemy threats so that they are rarely executed. His early games show a more aggressive style with more games being resolved by tactical means. Here is one of his most instructive and enjoyable creations.

ANATOLY KARPOV VS. GIK
Moscow, 1968
Sicilian Defense: Dragon Variation
**1.e4 c5; 2.Nf3 d6; 3.d4 cxd4; 4.Nxd4 Nf6; 5.Nc3 g6; 6.Be3 Bg7;
7.f3 Nc6; 8.Bc4 0-0; 9.Qd2 Qa5; 10.0-0-0.**

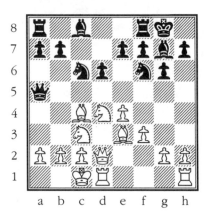

In his youth Karpov had no fear of tactical brawls, and the
Yugoslav Attack of the Sicilian Dragon was, at the time, one of the
wildest openings.

10...Bd7; 11.h4 Ne5; 12.Bb3 Rfc8. Attacks on both wings are
typical of the Dragon, and tactics usually accompany the action.
White will open the h-file, if possible, while Black plans to damage
the barrier with an exchange sacrifice at c3; **13.h5 Nxh5; 14.Bh6
Bxh6; 15.Qxh6 Rxc3; 16.bxc3 Qxc3.**

The course of the middlegame has been charted. Each side will go after the enemy king, using all the tactical devices at their disposal.

17.Ne2 Qc5. 17...Nd3+ is a trick that backfires. 18.Rxd3 Qa1+; 19.Kd2 Qxh1 grabs the exchange but the kingside gets demolished. 20.Bxf7+! The king is deflected from the defense of h7. 20...Kxf7; 21.Qxh7+ Kf6; 22.Nf4 and both d5 and g6 are under attack. Of course the knight cannot be captured because of the pin on the h-file.

18.g4 Nf6; 19.g5. At first, this move seems strange, because it allows the knight to get back to h5 and block the file. White intends to remove the defender of the kingside by the most brutal means. 19...Nh5; 20.Rxh5! This sacrifice was necessary, because Black had threats, too. 20.Ng3 runs into the spectacular 20...Bg4!; 21.fxg4 Nxg4 and White's queen is trapped!

20...gxh5.

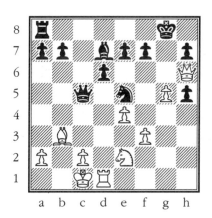

White has disrupted the pawn barrier and the weak pawns on the h-file will surely fall. In the meantime, Black has little to show on the queenside.

21.Rh1. White simply wants to get rid of the h-pawn and get at h7. **21...Qe3+; 22.Kb1 Qxf3.** 22...Ng6; 23.Qxh5 Nf8 doesn't defend because f7 is loose. 22...Qxe2 gets mated. 23.Qxh5 e6; 24.Qxh7+ Kf8; 25.Qh8+ Ke7; 26.Qf6+ Ke8; 27.Rh8#. **23.Rxh5 e6.**

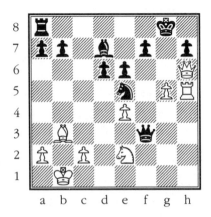

Black still has enough of a barrier to defend the king, but Karpov finds an amazing resource. 23...Qxe4 defends h7, but there are other tactical surprises in store for Black. 24.g6! The theme of the actual game is reflected in this variation. 24...Qxg6 is the only defense, but White pins the queen with 25.Rg5.

24.g6! Nxg6?! Not 24...hxg6; 25.Qh8#. 24...fxg6 was the best try. 25.Qxh7+ Kf8; 26.Qh8+ Ke7 (26...Kf7; 27.Rh7#) 27.Rh7+ Nf7; 28.Qxa8 Qxe2; 29.Qxb7 with the threat of Rxf7+ followed by Qxd7, with an extra piece. Black can defend with 29...Qf1+; 30.Kb2 Qf2 holding on to all the pieces. White has the exchange for a pawn, and can keep the initiative with 31.e5 dxe5; 32.Qb4+ Ke8; 33.Qb8+ Ke7; 34.Qxe5 with some winning chances if the c-pawn can get moving.

25.Qxh7+ Kf8.

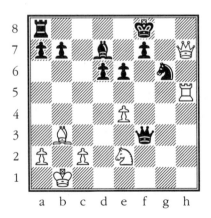

Black has two extra pawns, but Karpov has another shot, based on the pressure at f7.

26.Rf5!! The interference on the f-file forces Black to take desperate measures. **26...Qxb3+; 27.axb3 exf5.** There was no better defense, but the threat of check at h8 gives Karpov yet another tactic. 28.Nf4! Rd8. The rook moves to a square where it can be defended by the king.

29.Qh6+ Ke8; 30.Nxg6 fxg6; 31.Qxg6+ Ke7; 32.Qg5+ Ke833.exf5 Rc8; 34.Qg8+ Ke7; 35.Qg7+. Black resigned, as defeat is the inevitable result of the advance of the f-pawn.

21. GARRY KASPAROV

Thirteenth World Champion
(1985-1993, PCA/WCC 1993-present)

Garry Kasparov is widely recognized as the greatest player chess has ever known. He has been a dominating presence on the tournament scene for almost two decades. After wresting the title from Karpov in 1985, he has defended it against top challengers, though outside the umbrella of the World Chess Federation.

Kasparov's style is uncompromising. He can attack like Tal, investing material speculatively, or play pressure chess, increasing the tension until the enemy breaks down. He takes more risks than most World Champions, trusting his technique to navigate the dangerous waters of the middlegame. His games display many great tactics, and the side variations in his published analyis is no less fascinating.

Kasparov has been the undisputed top player in the world for over a dozen years. His two closest rivals are Viswanathan Anand and Vladimir Kramnik. In our game, Anand gets a tactical lesson, reminding him that he must work even harder to unseat the reigning champ. Kasparov adopts a rare gambit to set the stage for the tactics.

GARRY KASPAROV VS. ANAND
Tal Memorial, Riga, Latvia, 1995
Evans Gambit
1.e4 e5; 2.Nf3 Nc6; 3.Bc4 Bc5; 4.b4 Bxb4.

The ancient Evans Gambit is rejuvenated in the hands of the World Champion. Tying together the old opening and latest superstars seems a fitting way to end our survey of the tactics of the World Champions.

5.c3 Be7; 6.d4 Na5; 7.Be2!? exd4; 8.Qxd4! A new approach at the time. **8...Nf6?!** Black should creates some breathing room by advancing the d-pawn, for example 8...d6; 9.Qxg7 Bf6; 10.Qg3 Nc6; 11.0-0 Qe7 with a more sold position for Black. Opposite wing castling is likely. **9.e5 Nc6.** An intermezzo to get the knight back to a useful square. **10.Qh4 Nd5; 11.Qg3.**

11...g6. A necessary concession, weakening the dark squares. Castling was out of the question. 11...0-0?!; 12.Bh6 g6 might be playable if White gives up the beautiful bishop for the rook, but Kasparov intended to continue the attack with 13.h4!?

12.0-0 Nb6. Castling was still dangerous. 12...0-0; 13.Bh6 Re8; 14.c4Nb6; 15.Nc3 d6; 16.Rad1. The pin ties down Black's position. 16...Nd7; 17.Ng5! dxe5 (17...Ndxe5; 18.f4); 18.f4 was Kasparov's plan, the point being that 18...Bc5+; 19.Kh1 Bd4; 20.fxe5 Bxe5, which forks the knight and queen, runs into the clever reply 21.Qf3!, since 21...Qf6 leads to the win of the f-pawn after 22.Qe3! **13.c4.**

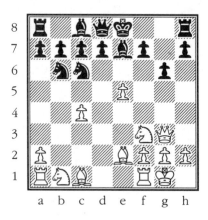

If only Black could castle! **13...d6.** 13...0-0; 14.Bh6 Re8; 15.Nc3 d6 transposes to the note on 12...0-0. **14.Rd1.** The pin is established.

14...Nd7. 14...Be6; 15.c5 (if 15.Qf4 Qc8!; 16.Bb2 Na4!, Black is in better shape, but not 15...0-0?; 16.Qh6 with White being clearly better) Nd5; 16.exd6 cxd6; 17.Bc4 Bf6; 18.Bg5 dxc5; 19.Nc3 Nxc3; 20.Rxd8+ Bxd8; 21.Re1! 0-0; 22.Qd6!

15.Bh6!

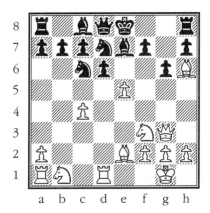

White has sacrificed one pawn and is willing to give up another at e5. Black is unable to castle, however, and despite the cluster of Black pieces surrounding the king, has no real defense at f7.

15...Ncxe5. It doesn't matter which knight Black uses, in the end f7 is defended. Kasparov shows why taking with the pawn would have been bad. 15...dxe5; 16.Nc3 Bf8 and now instead of 17.Bg5 what is really unclear after Be7; 18.Nd5 f6!; 19.Bh6 Bf8; 20.Be3 Kf7. 17.Qh3! deserves attention: 17...Bxh6 (or 17...Qe7; 18.Nd5 is terrible for Black) 18.Qxh6 f6; 19.Qg7 Rf8; 20.c5! with powerful pressure (threatening 21.Bc4). If 18...Qe7; 19.Nd5 Qd6; 20.c5! Nxc5; 21.Qg7 Rf8; 22.Nf6+ wins.

On the other hand, 17...f6. Interposing the bishop would just give White two free tempi to get the knight to d5. 18.Be3 Bg7; 19.c5! liberating the c4-square. 19...0-0; 20.Bc4+ Kh8; 21.Nh4! Threatens to destroy the barrier with a sacrifice at g6, so Black must defend 21...Qe8 (21...Ne7!?). 22.Nb5 sets up a fork at c7. Black can try 22...f5; 23.Nxc7 f4.

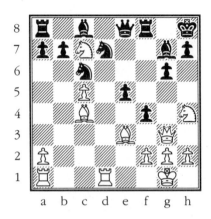

The counter-fork at f4 complicates matters greatly. White's best seems to be 24.Qg4 even though that walks into the discovered attack 24...Nf6 which forces the queen to retreat with 25.Qe2. Black can keep up the attack with 25...Bg4 which clears an escape path for the queen.

26.f3 Qb8; 27.Nxa8 fxe3; 28.fxg4 Qxa8; 29.g5! Nh5. After the tactics die down, White has the exchange for a pawn. Black's position is very weak, and the pawn at e3 falls quickly. 30.Rd6 Nd4 can be countered by 31.Qxe3 as the fork 31...Nc2 can be handled with 32.Nxg6+ hxg6; 33.Qh3. Black can avoid disaster by entering the endgame and creating a threat of capturing the c-pawn with check, forking the rook at d6. 33...Qc8!; 34.Qxc8 Rxc8; 35.Rc1 Nd4; 36.Rf1 Rxc5!?; 37.Rd8+ Kh7; 38.Bg8+ Kh8 with a draw by repetition. 22.Nd5 Nxd5. Kasparov now planned the destructive intermezzo 23.Nxg6+! hxg6 and only then 24.Bxd5, after which Black gets clobbered on the h-file, for example 24...Bh6; 25.Qh4 Qe7; 26.Qxh6+ Qh7; 27.Qxh7+ Kxh7; 28.c6! with a new threatened fork at b7. 28...bxc6; 29.Bxc6 is yet another fork, and Black must lose significant material.

Returning to the game, Kasparov played **16.Nxe5.**

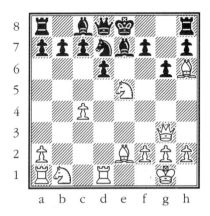

16...Nxe5. This time the refutation of the pawn capture is simpler. 16...dxe5; 17.Nc3 c6, taking control over the key square d5. The game may continue with 18.Ne4 Qc7; 19.Bg7 Rg8; 20.Rxd7!? Qxd7; 21.Qxe5 Qe6; 22.Qd4 c5; 23.Qc3 Qxe4; 24.Bf3.

White has sufficient compensation for the exchange, that is, a great superiority for development.

16...Nxe5; 17.Nc3 Nd7; 18.Ne4 Bf8; 19.Qc3 Rg8; 20.Qe3 Qe7; 21.Bg5 Qe6; 22.Bg4! f5; 23.Nxd6+, mating in two moves.

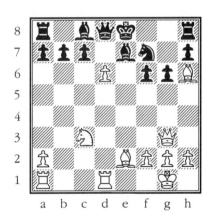

19...cxd6. 19...Bxd6 isn't any better. 20.Bb5+ is tough to meet. 20...c6; 21.Bf4 is a win because 21...cxb5 (21...Ke7; 22.Ne4 Bxf4; 23.Qxf4 and the threat at f6 dooms the Black queen.) 22.Bxd6 Nxd6; 23.Rxd6. Black can't play 20...Bd7; 21.Re1+ Be5 (21...Ne5; 22.Bc4 with the horrible threat of f4.) 22.Bg7 Rg8; 23.Bxd7+ Kxd7. (23...Qxd7; 24.Bxf6 wins a piece.) 24.Qh3+.

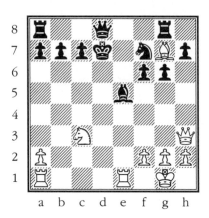

There are two tries here. 24...Kc6 is met by 25.Rac1! There are deadly consequences to White's discovered check, unless the king finds shelter. 25...b6 (25...Rxg7; 26.Ne4+ forces mate.) 26.Qe6+ Nd6; 27.Nd5+ Kb7; 28.Rxc7+ forces Black to get what he can for the queen with 28...Qxc7; 29.Nxc7 Kxc7 but after 30.Bxf6 Bxf6; 31.Qxf6 Black doesn't have enough, and it is not easy to hold on to what he has. The other plan is 24...Ke7; 25.Qxh7 Qd4; 26.Rac1! (26.Ne4 Qxa1; 27.Rxa1 Bxa1; 28.Qxg6 allows a clever defense with 28...Rae8! because 29.Bxf6+ Kf8!! is a discovered attack against the White knight, which is pinned to a back rank mate.

White's queen and bishop are also attacked, and there are no checks to be given.) 26...Ng5; 27.Qxg6 Ne6 generates counterplay, because the bishop at g7 is pinned and apparently lost.

White has a win based on the fork at d5 which seems to be out of the question. It is just a matter of getting the queen out of the way, and this needs a double deflection! 28.Rxe5!! Qxe5 (28...fxe5; 29.Qf6+ Kd7; 30.Qf7+ wins.) 29.Bxf6+!! A deflection and a decoy! 29...Qxf6; 30.Nd5+ Kd6; 31.Qxf6 Kxd5; 32.Rd1+. Black will be checkmated.

In any case, the game continued **20.Qe3!**

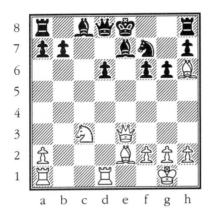

The pin on the e-file is worth the bishop at h6. **20...Nxh6.** 20...Qb6 might have been wiser. 21.Bb5+ Bd7 (21...Kd8; 22.Qe2 Nxh6; 23.Nd5 is a fork that creates a mate threat at e7.); 22.Bxd7+ Kxd7; 23.Qh3+ f5; 24.Nd5 gives White an attack, according to Kasparov.

21.Qxh6 Bf8; 22.Qe3+! Back to the e-file!

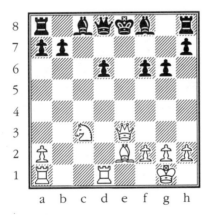

22...Kf7; 23.Nd5. White blocks the d-pawn, thereby suffocating Black's position, as well as preserving an eventual threat of Bc4 followed by discovered check. **23...Be6?!** 23...Bg7 looks appealing, but it fails. 24.Bc4 Be6; 25.Bb3! Re8; 26.Nf4 d5; 27.Nxe6 Rxe6; 28.Rxd5!

An amazing position reached in analysis by Kasparov. There is much to be discovered here. 28...Rxe3. (28...Qb6; 29.Rd7+ Kf8; 30.Qxe6 Qxe6; 31.Bxe6 gives White an extra rook.) 29.Rxd8+ discovered check, and a new attack at a8. 29...Rxb3; 30.Rxa8 Rb2; 31.Rxa7. White is up the exchange. 23...Bd7 was the best defense. 24.Rac1 Bc6; 25.Bc4 Kg7; 26.Nf4 Bd7; 27.Bd5 is nevertheless very uncomfortable for Black.

Back to the game, the action continued with **24.Nf4! Qe7.**

Black is almost out of the woods, but Kasparov has a subtle but effective move which sets up an awesome threat.

25.Re1! Black resigned. The basic threat is Bf3 followed by Nxe6 and then Bf5. 25...Bh6 (25...Bh6 d5; 26.Bf3 Bh6 is similar); 26.Bc4!! takes advantage of the pin on the e-file. 26...d5; 27.Bxd5 Rad8;

28.Nxe6!! Bxe3; 29.Nxd8+. Discovered check wins a rook and two pieces for the queen. 29...Kg7; 30.Ne6+ Kf7 30...Kh6; 31.Rxe3 threatens mate at h3. 31...g5; 32.Nxg5 is a discovered attack on the queen, and a fork is coming at f7. 31.Rxe3 Qd6; 32.Rc1 continues the assault. 32...Qxd5; 33.Rc7+ Ke8; 34.Nf4+ Qe5; 35.Rxe5+ fxe5; 36.Rc8+ and White wins.

We've seen how the World Champions used tactics to earn valuable points in tournament play, and to impress the crowd with dazzling fireworks. Now it is your turn. Imagine that you can somehow achieve the positional advantages which make possible tactical victories. A long section of quizzes based on actual positions from World Champion games awaits you in the next chapter.

22. QUIZZES

Each of the quiz positions comes with a hint. Some of them are very easy, others require moves even masters fail to spot. You should look at each diagram in terms of the tactics presented in this book. Look for actual or potential pins, forks, skewers, discovered attacks, discovered checks, etc. Whenever you see that the enemy king may use an escape route, try to choke it. Demolish protective barriers as if they were mere tissues. In short, work hard and have fun!

MORPHY VS. MORPHY
New Orleans, 1849

This is one of the earliest games we have for Morphy, played against Alonzo Morphy, his father. Many players would play Re1+ here, but Morphy notices action elsewhere that is more effective. Use a deflection sacrifice to win quickly.

MORPHY VS. AYERS
Mobile, 1855

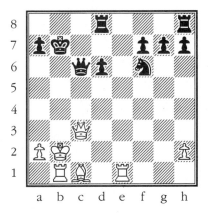

Find the discovered check that led to victory!

SCHULTEN VS. MORPHY
New York, 1857

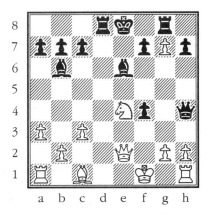

You can pin the queen by bringing the bishop to c4, but is that your best move? Morphy found the killer move.

PAULSEN VS. MORPHY
New York, 1857

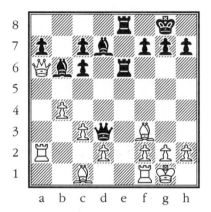

This is one of Morphy's most famous combinations. To solve it, you'll need to destroy the barrier and then set up a discovered check. It takes a few moves, but if you choose wisely, victory is inevitable. Morphy even played a second-best move at one point, so perfection is not needed.

MORPHY VS. CARR
Blindfold Game, 1858

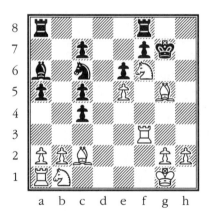

Decoy the king to an open file, then finish it off in six moves or less.

MORPHY VS. JOUNOUD
Paris, 1858

Black has an overworked queen. Make the most of it!

MORPHY VS. CUNNINGHAM
Blindfold Game, 1859

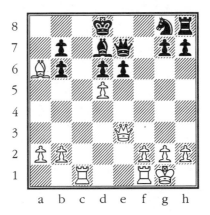

White has already sacrificed a piece, and the Black king can escape via e8 to a relatively safe square at f7. White can take the b-pawn with check and win another pawn, but there is a stronger move, involving a decoy.

STEINITZ VS. DE VERE
Paris, 1867

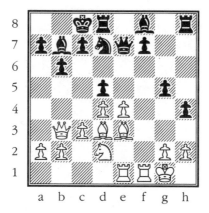

Finding the best move here isn't rocket science. The question is, can you identify all of the relevant tactics. When Steinitz played his move, De Vere resigned!

LASKER VS. CAPABLANCA
St. Petersburg, 1914

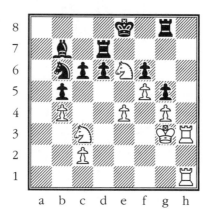

How do you get the knight at c3 into the attack?

EUWE VS. MAROCZY
Match, Amsterdam, 1921

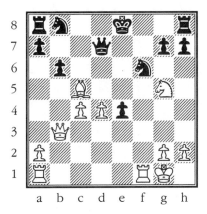

If the Black knight at f6 were a White one instead, wouldn't that be nice. Make it so!

CAPABLANCA VS. BOGOLJUBOW
Match, London, 1922

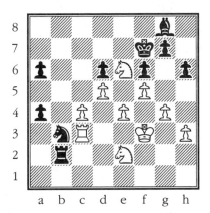

The position is so blocked that White can't get an attack going, and Black's a-pawn is flying down the board. Capablanca found a way to open lines, can you?

WALTER VS. LASKER
Mahrisch Ostrau, 1923

Deflection leads to resignation.

CAPABLANCA VS. JANOWSKI
New York, 1924

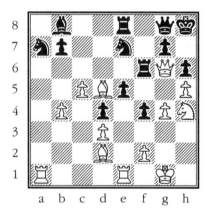

The queen at g6 is almost trapped, and if it retreats to e4 the bishop at d5 falls. Turn it into a desperado and win!

KUPCHIK VS. CAPABLANCA
Lake Hopaton, 1926

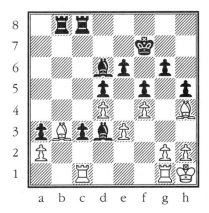

Use a small sacrifice to entrap a White rook, then trap the other one!

RETI VS. CAPABLANCA
Berlin, 1928

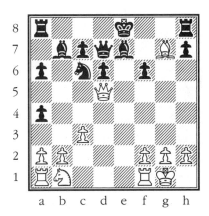

White is attacking with queen and bishop, but that is about it. Black doesn't seem to be attacking at all. How quickly things can change! How did Capablanca turn this game into a miniature?

STAHLBERG VS. ALEKHINE
Hamburg Olympiad, 1930

White has almost all the pieces involved in the defense, but the barrier still falls.

NAEGELI VS. EUWE
Bern, 1932

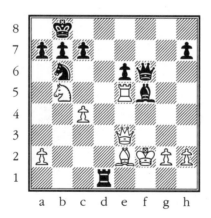

What's the best discovered check?

QUIZZES

BOTVINNIK VS. SPIELMANN
Moscow, 1935

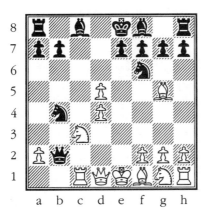

Trap the enemy queen!

LASKER VS. LEVENFISH
Moscow, 1936

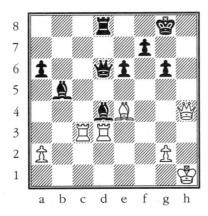

White's brilliant destruction of the barrier is rejected by most computers, but Lasker had it all worked out. Are you man, or machine?

EUWE VS. TARTAKOWER
Nottingham, 1936

Forks are lying around all over the place. Pick the right ones, make them happen, and win.

ALEKHINE VS. RESHEVSKY
Kemeri, 1937

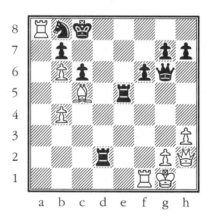

Use a decoy tactic to set up a clearance tactic, and deliver checkmate.

BOTVINNIK VS. CAPABLANCA
Rotterdam, 1938

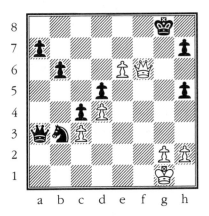

This position has been analyzed many times, but the tactics run deeper than many people have appreciated. The key is the control of f8, as White threatens Qf7+ and Qf8# if the square is not under Black control. White has a few ways to proceed, and Botvinnik didn't find the most efficient win. The tactic we are concerned with here is pursuit. Black must not be allowed to perpetually harass the White king. So it is up to you: advance the pawn or check at f7?

ALEKHINE VS. KIENINGER
Poland, 1941

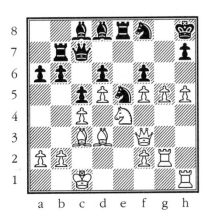

Alekhine's queen is attacked. Did he spare a thought for the lady? Should you?

BOTVINNIK VS. RAGOZIN
Leningrad (match), 1940

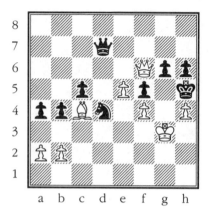

White wants to play Be2 and deliver checkmate, but the pesky knight defends that square. How did Botvinnik get rid of it?

ALEKHINE VS. RETHY
Munich, 1941

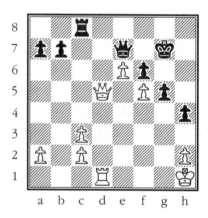

White wins by creating a pin, and then clearing the key square for another piece.

DENKER VS. BOTVINNIK
USA vs. Soviet Union, 1945

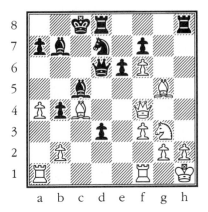

The bishop at c5 already chokes the g1 square so all you need to do is open the kingside.

SMYSLOV VS. KAMYSHOV
Moscow City Championship, 1945

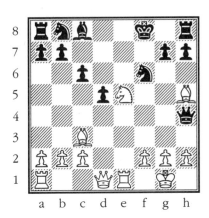

This is a tough one, and computers can chew on it for a while without finding the solution that Smyslov found. The key is the e8 square. Forks play a major part in the action. Start by setting a trap that involves one.

PETROSIAN VS. KOROLKOV
Tbilisi, 1945

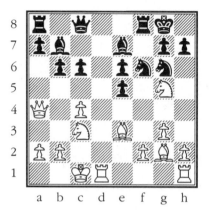

Here's an easy one. Its all about pins.

SMYSLOV VS. RUDAKOWSKY
Soviet Championship, 1945

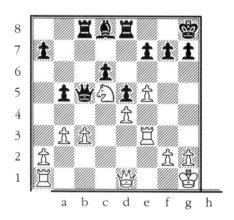

Your task here is to crack the pawn barrier and get your heavy pieces into position to wipe out the kingside.

SPASSKY VS. AFTONOV
Leningrad, 1949

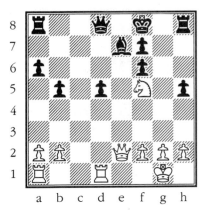

The idle rooks place the entire defensive burden on the queen at d8.

BOTVINNIK VS. SMYSLOV
World Championship, 1954

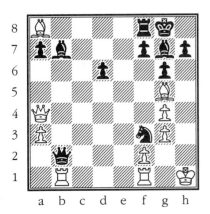

A glance at the board shows Black with the possibility of a discovered check, but the bishop at b7 is not only under attack from its opposite number at a8, it also is x-rayed from b1. Establish Black's priorities and find the best move.

EUWE VS. FISCHER
New York, 1957

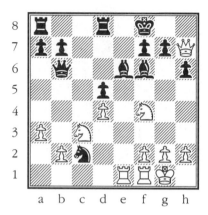

Back has just captured a bishop at c2 and anticipates White's recapture with the queen. Instead, young Fischer gets mated by Euwe.

TAL VS. KLIAVINS
Latvian Teams Championship, 1958

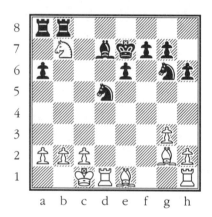

Material is even, and the Black king seems to be safe. The hanging knight at b7 should give Black the initiative, but Tal refused to retreat. What did he do instead?

TAL VS. NEI
Soviet Union, 1958

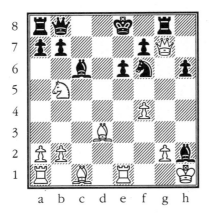

Finish off the king by deflecting a key defender.

NIEMALA VS. SPASSKY
Riga, 1959

Black could win eventually with the passive Raa6, but by using a deflection Black can consolidate his advantage more quickly. How did Spassky do it?

PETROSIAN VS. NIELSEN
Copenhagen, 1960

Start with a decoy, trap a rook, and win with a final fork.

UNZICKER VS. TAL
W. Germany vs. Soviet Union, 1960

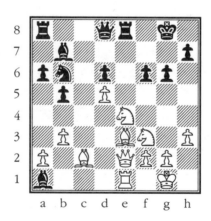

White expected Tal to retreat the bishop, but he forced a win by relying on the power of the rook at e8. How did he take advantage of the pile of pieces on the e-file?

LETELIER VS. FISCHER
Leipzig Olympiad, 1960

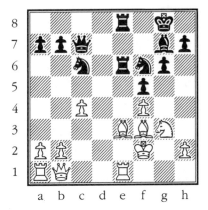

Three-time U.S. Champion, 17-year-old Bobby Fischer treats this game like a veteran pro. The tail-end sacrifice is stupendous and amusing. First, bring the White king a little closer to the center.

NYEZHMETDINOV VS. TAL
Baku, 1961

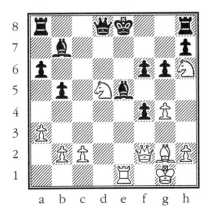

Remove a defender, pile pressure on a pin, use a check to create a discovered attack, and force the Black king to march into a pin!

PETROSIAN VS. PACHMAN
Bled, 1961

Black's king is not well defended, but White is only attacking with the queen. She packs quite a punch!

TAL VS. BOTVINNIK
World Championship, 1961

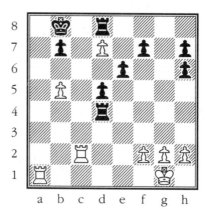

A double-decoy earns you a promotion!

TAL VS. GHITESCU
Miskolcz, 1963

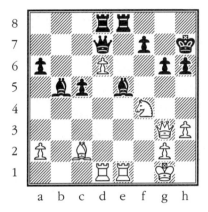

Destroy the defenders of Black's king and win!

FISCHER VS. SUTTLES
United States Championship, 1965

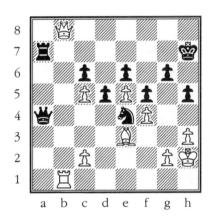

Choke the king and complete the mating net as quickly as possible.

SPASSKY VS. LANGEWEG
Sochi,1967

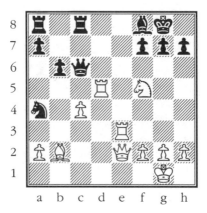

What is the best way to destroy the barrier?

PETROSIAN VS. SPASSKY
World Championship, 1969

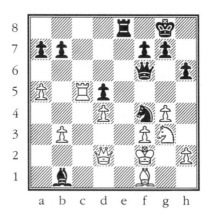

Use an interference to set up threats that White simply cannot cope with.

LARSEN VS. TAL
Candidates Match, 1969

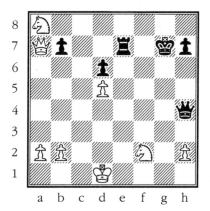

A wide open position, with White's pieces flung to the distant corners of the universe. Can the two Black pieces converge to deliver mate? The king has three flight squares. Choke him down to one!

FISCHER VS. SCHWEBER
Buenos Aires, 1970

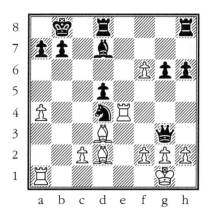

The previous moves saw White's rook capturing at e4, and Black responding to a threatened pin from f4 by taking the White queen at g3. Fischer had no intention of recapturing, which would have left him at a disadvantage after Black captures the rook at e4. Instead, he had a shocking intermezzo. What was it?

ALBURT VS. TAL
Soviet Championship, 1972

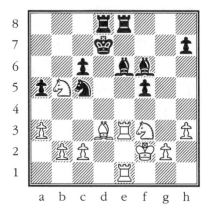

White just offered up the knight by capturing a pawn at b5, appreciating that if Black captures, the rook on e8 gets skewered. Tal responded with an intermezzo that quickly turned the tide. What was it?

TAL VS. CASTRO
Interzonal Biel, 1976

Black has two pawns for a piece. The pin on the diagonal preserves the knight. White's bishop at c2 has no scope. Are things all that bad for Black? They are indeed, and it is a double attack that brings White a decisive advantage. Force the win!

PETROSIAN VS. ALBURT
Soviet Championship, 1977

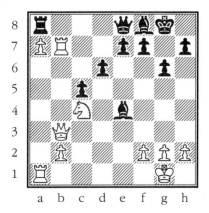

The promotion of the pawn doesn't look very promising right now, but you can change that with one good move.

SIBAREVIC VS. KASPAROV
Banja Luka, 1979

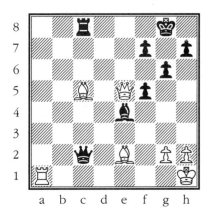

White has just captured at c5 and is a piece ahead. Black can capture either White bishop, and with the extra pawns can probably win in any case. What is the best move?

KASPAROV VS. LIGTERINK
Malta Olympiad, 1980

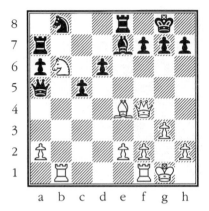

That the knight will move, creating a discovered attack, is taken for granted. But where?

KASPAROV VS. KUIJPERS
Dortmund, 1980

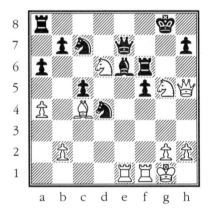

The pin on the e-file can be used to obtain a winning advantage. Remember, Black is up a pawn so you have to be efficient!

KARPOV VS. ALBURT
Malta Olympiad, 1980

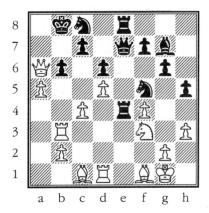

How did Karpov destroy the wall? You'll need to clear some territory.

KAVALEK VS. KASPAROV
Bugojno, 1982

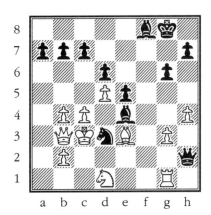

Kasparov puts the knight to good use, setting up a big fork.

TIMMAN VS. KASPAROV
Bugojno, 1982

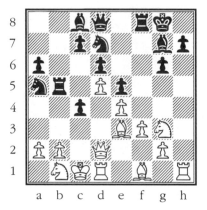

Black's queenside seems roomy enough, but there is a way to trap a piece. Can you find it?

ALBURT VS. KASPAROV
Lucerne Olympiad 1982

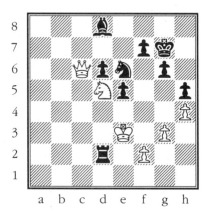

White's last move, 51.Ke3, was a blunder and it allows Kasparov to win by setting up a fork. How?

NIKOLIC VS. KASPAROV
Niksic, 1983

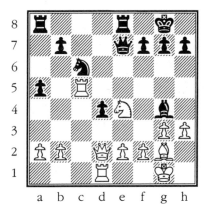

Exploit a pin to win a pawn!

KASPAROV VS. IVANCHUK
Soviet Championship, 1988

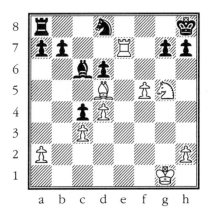

If only the rook could get to h7!

KARPOV VS. MALANIUK
Soviet Championship, 1988

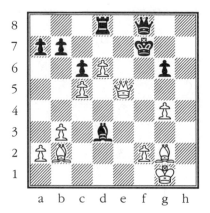

Take advantage of the hapless king to force mate.

SMYSLOV VS. BLACKSTOCK
London (Lloyds Bank), 1988

Deflection opens a key line and enables a checkmate.

KARPOV VS. NIKOLIC
Skelleftea, 1989

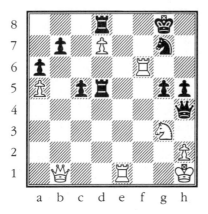

Black is threatening to grab the pawn at d7. While the pawn stands, it can be put to good use! What is your suggestion for White?

FISCHER VS. SPASSKY
Match, 1992

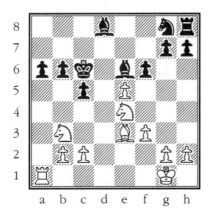

Spassky took into account captures at a6 and f6, but there was a destructive force he didn't reckon on. What is it?

SPASSKY VS. FISCHER
Match, 1992

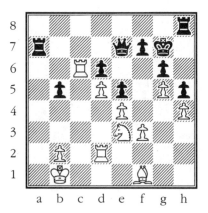

Decoy, fork, set up a double attack. Just a routine day at the office for Fischer. And for you? Don't settle for slow methods!

CHABANON VS. KASPAROV
French Team Championship, 1993

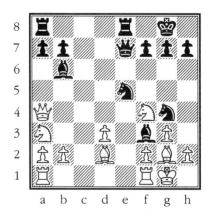

Black's pieces are swarming around the enemy position, but how do you break down the door and get to the goodies?

QUIZZES

KASPAROV VS. SHORT
Amsterdam (Euwe Memorial), 1994

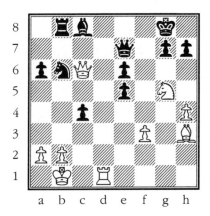

White is piling on the pawn at e6, but has to worry a little about Black's queenside counterplay. Using a double attack, Kasparov manages to win both e-pawns! How did he manage that?

KARPOV VS. GEORGIEV
Tilburg, 1994

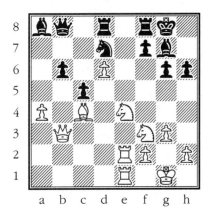

The Black king has a rook, bishop and three pawns as defenders, with the knight at d7 assisting. White attacks with just queen and bishop, as the knights are targeted by the bishop at a8. Nevertheless, White can destroy the defense. How?

LAUTIER VS. KARPOV
Linares, 1995

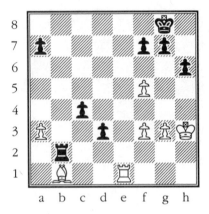

Black has two advanced pawns for the piece. Chart the fastest course to promotion!

DEEP BLUE VS. KASPAROV
Man vs. Machine, 1997

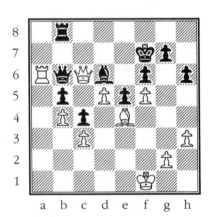

In the famous match against a supercomputer, Kasparov resigned in a position which should have been drawn. Can you find the correct plan, involving perpetual check?

23. SOLUTIONS TO THE QUIZZES

Here you will find the answer to each of the quiz positions in the previous chapter. We've repeated the initial position, but without the hints, so if you want a tougher challenge just start here and cover up the solutions.

MORPHY VS. MORPHY
New Orleans, 1849

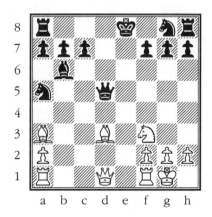

Solution: 15.Bb5+!

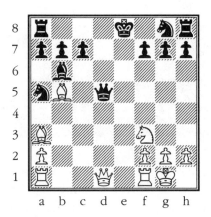

The queen is deflected, and the White queen now controls the d-file.. 15.Re1+ Kd8 is not as easy to crack.

15...Qxb5; 16.Re1+ Ne7.

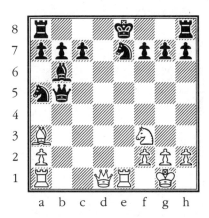

Sometimes the possibility to play brilliantly overcomes common sense. In the 19th century a premium was put on artistic moves, so perhaps Morphy was inclined to make things interesting.

17.Rb1. A little too fancy. Simply capturing at e7 was most efficient. 17.Rxe7+ Kf8 tempts White to use the discovered check immediately, but patience brings greater rewards. 18.Rb1! Qa6. Morphy could then have destroyed the pawn barrier with a brilliant rook sacrifice. 19.Rxf7+!! Kxf7; 20.Qd7+ Kf6; 21.Be7+ Kg6; 22.Qe6+

Kh5; 23.g4#. **17...Qa6??** Black walks into mate in 6. 17...Qd7! How could Black miss this obvious defense?; 18.Qxd7+ Kxd7; 19.Rxe7+ Kc8; 20.Rxf7 provides compensation for the pawn, but not much more.

18.Rxe7+ Kf8; 19.Qd5 Qc4; 20.Rxf7+ Kg8; 21.Rf8#.

MORPHY VS. AYERS
Mobile, 1855

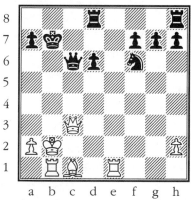

Solution: 23.Ka1+!

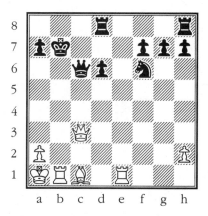

23.Ka3+ Kc7; 24.Qa5+ Kc8; 25.Qxa7 doesn't work now, because of 25...Qc5+. 23.Kc2+ Kc7 pins the White queen.

23...Kc7; 24.Qa5+ Kc8. 24...Kd7; 25.Qxa7+ Qc7; 26.Rb7 Ne8; 27.Rxe8 Qxb7; 28.Rxd8+! **25.Qxa7 Nd7; 26.Bd2.** Black resigned. A rook is coming to c1. 26...Qc7 loses to 27.Qa6+ and mate next.

SCHULTEN VS. MORPHY
New York, 1857

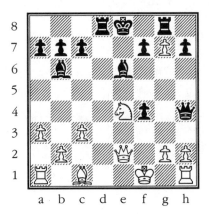

Solution: 17...Rd1+!!

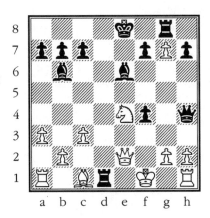

The queen is deflected from its excellent defensive post. 17...Bc4?? 18.Nf6# is discovered checkmate!

18.Qxd1 Bc4+. Caught in the crossfire on the diagonals, White would have to give up the queen. **19.Qe2 Bxe2+; 20.Kxe2 f5** drives the knight back to d2, and after **21.Nd2 Qf2+; 22.Kd1 Rxg7** White has no reason to play on.

PAULSEN VS. MORPHY
New York, 1857

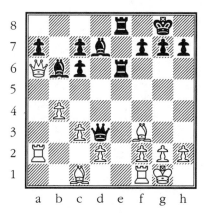

Solution: 17...Qxf3!!

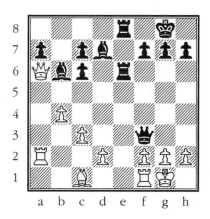

18.gxf3 Rg6+; 19.Kh1 Bh3. The threat is 20...Bg2+; 21.Kg1 Bxf3 mate. **20.Rd1 Bg2+; 21.Kg1 Bxf3+; 22.Kf1.** Here Morphy actually missed a quicker win.

22...Bg2+? 22...Rg2! threatens Rxh2 and Rh1#. 23.Qd3 Rxf2+; 24.Kg1 Rg2+; 25.Kh1 Rg1# would be an elegant discovered checkmate! **23.Kg1 Bh3+; 24.Kh1 Bxf2; 25.Qf1.** The only defense to the dual mate threats of ...Rg1 and ...Bg2. 25...Bxf1 and Black went on to win.

MORPHY VS. CARR
Blindfold Game, 1858

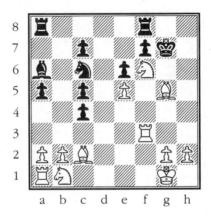

Solution: 20.Bh6+!

The bishop was only in the way.

20...Kxh6; 21.Rh3+ Kg5; 22.Rh5+ Kf4; 23.Kf2! The finishing touch. White will checkmate with a lowly pawn. **23...Rg8; 24.g3+ Rxg3; 25.hxg3#.**

MORPHY VS. JOUNOUD
Paris, 1858

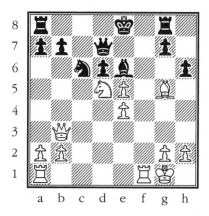

Solution: 16.Nc7+!

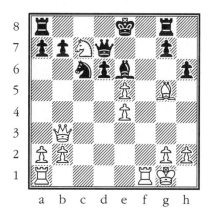

The knight must be captured, there is no alternative.

16...Qxc7; 17.Qxe6+. Black resigned. 17...Ne7; 18.Bxe7 Qxe7; 19.Qxg8+ etc.

MORPHY VS. CUNNINGHAM
Blindfold Game, 1859

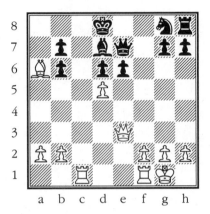

Solution: 21.Bb5!

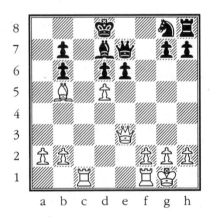

This is not an easy move to find, because it is not immediately clear how capturing the bishop worsens Black's position. It is a case of removing the defender, since if Black captures, White will regain the piece after a check at b6, and then the path to victory is clear.

21...Ke8. 21...Bxb5 allows 22.Qxb6+ Ke8; 23.Qxb5+ Kf7; 24.dxe6+! Qxe6 (24...Kf8; 25.Rc8+ 24...Kf6; 25.Rfe1 is hopeless for Black.); 25.Rfe1 Qf6; 26.Qd7+ Ne7; 27.Rc3. The rook lift threatens Rf3, pinning and winning the Black queen, which cannot run away now because the knight at e7 will be lost, for example 27...Qg5; 28.Qe6+! Kf8; 29.Rc8+. The deflection enables the checkmate.

29...Nxc8; 30.Qe8#. **22.dxe6.**

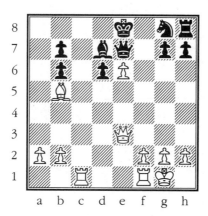

A choke is applied to f7. Now Rc7+ will win. The game continued **22...Nf6.** The pawn cannot be captured because of the pin on the bishop at d7. 22...Bc6; 23.Bxc6+ bxc6; 24.Rxc6 is a simple win.

23.Rc8+. One final exploitation of the pin at d7 forces Black's capitulation.

STEINITZ VS. DE VERE
Paris, 1867

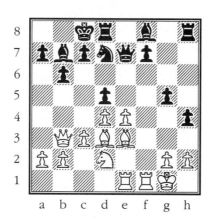

Solution: 16.exd5!

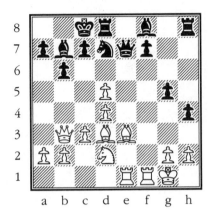

The move is obvious enough, as White captures a pawn for free. De Vere resigned, but not because of the pawn. Black has no defense against the threat of d6 followed by Rxf7.

Let's look at some of the possibilities.

16...Nf6; 17.Bxg5 wins at least a piece.

16...Qd6; 17.Bxg5 wins because the rook is choked, and 17...f6 loses to 18.Ne4 Qxd5; 19.Qxd5 Bxd5; 20.Nxf6.

16...h3!?; 17.Bf4 hg2; 18.Rxe7 gxf1 (Q) + 19.Bxf1 Bxe7; 20.Bg3 Nc5!; 21.dxc5 Bxc5+; 22.Bf2 Bxd5; 23.c4 Rxh2+; 24.Kg3 Rxd2; 25.cxd5 R8xd5. Black's chances are slightly better. The main line is 18.Kxg2 gxf4; 19.Rxe7 Bxe7; 20.Nf3 Nf6; 21.c4 Rdg8+; 22.Kh1 Nh5 which really gives Black serious counterplay. 23.Rf2 Ng3; 24.Kg2 Ne4+; 25.Kf1 Nxf2; 26.Kxf2 c5! for example 27.dxc5 Bxc5+; 28.Kf1 Kc7; 29.Bf5 Rxh2!; 30.Nxh2 Rg1+; 31.Ke2 Rg2+ draws. 27.dxc6 Bxc6; 28.d5 Bc5+; 29.Kf1 Bd7 where White is in trouble.

LASKER VS. CAPABLANCA
St.Petersburg, 1914

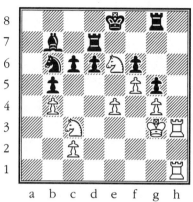

Solution: 35.e5!

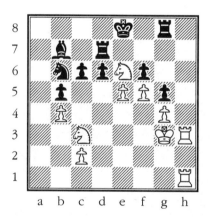

A clearance move which liberates the d4 square for use by the knight.

35...dxe5; 36.Ne4. The f6-square must be defended. **36...Nd5; 37.N6c5.** A fork is applied to the rook and bishop, but if the rook stays on the seventh rank, then a new fork scoops up a piece. **37...Bc8.** 37...Rc7; 38.Nxb7 Rxb7; 39.Nd6+ gives White an extra rook.

38.Nxd7 Bxd7; 39.Rh7. White has the exchange for a pawn, which might not be winning except that Black's bishop is suffocated.

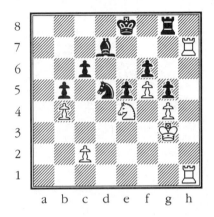

39...Rf8; 40.Ra1. Threatening a back rank mate.

40...Kd8; 41.Ra8+ Bc8 defends, but **42.Nc5** caused resignation as Black cannot defend against the dual threats of Nc7+ and Ne6+.

EUWE VS. MAROCZY
Match, Amsterdam, 1921

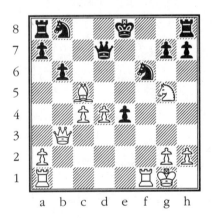

Solution: 20.Rxf6!!

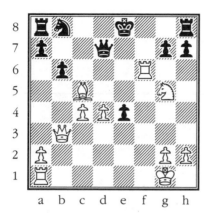

The enemy knight is removed. **20...gxf6; 21.Nxe4.** The threat is now Nxf6+.

21...Qe6. The pawn is defended, but the king and queen are in an unfortunate alignment for Black.

22.Re1. Re-establishing the threat, and now Black has no useful defense. **22...bxc5; 23.Nxf6+ Kf7; 24.Qb7+.** This intermezzo before capturing the Black queen is the most efficient win.

CAPABLANCA VS. BOGOLJUBOW
Match, London, 1922

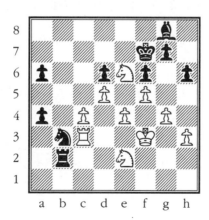

Solution: 42.c5!!

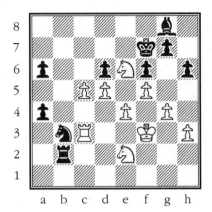

Black must take the pawn, because otherwise it grows into a queen in a few moves.

42...dxc5. 42...Nxc5; 43.Nxc5 dxc5; 44.Rxc5 and White has no problems coping with the a-pawns, and the d-pawn should win. **43.Nxc5 Nd2+.** 43...Nxc5; 44.Rxc5 transposes to the previous note.

44.Kf2 Ke7?! There was a better defense. 44...Nb1!; 45.Rc4! a3; 46.Ne6! Ke7! (46...a2; 47.Rc7+ Ke8; 48.d6 with a mating net.) 47.Rc7+ Kd6; 48.Rc6+ Ke7; 49.Rxa6 (49.Rc7+ Kd6 draws.) 49...Bxe6 It has been suggested that Black is okay here, but that was on the assumption that White had to take at e6 with the rook. 50.fxe6! (50.Rxe6+ Kd7; 51.Ra6 a2; 52.Ke1 and the king gets over in time.) 50...Nc3. Black wins the knight, but that doesn't matter. 51.Ra7+ Ke8; 52.Ke3! Rxe2+. (52...Nxe2; 53.d6 builds the mating net. 52...Nxe4; 53.Nd4! All eyes remain on mate.) 53.Kd3 Rxe4; 54.Kxc3 and Black cannot hold.

45.Ke1 Nb1; 46.Rd3 a3?! and here Black should have stuck to his plan, instead of belatedly switching to the queenside advance. 46...Kd6!; 47.Nxa4 Rb4; 48.Nac3 Nxc3; 49.Nxc3 Bf7; 50.Kd2 g6; 51.Ke3 gxf5; 52.gxf5 Be8 with drawing chances, although the kingside pawns remain very weak. **47.d6+ Kd8.**

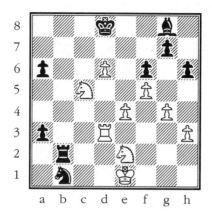

At this point White is concentrating on mate rather than a longwinded endgame. The idea is that a knight at c6 would force the king off the queening square.

48.Nd4! Rb6; 49.Nde6+ Bxe6; 50.fxe6 Rb8; 51.e7+ Ke8; 52.Nxa6. Black resigned.

WALTER VS. LASKER
Mahrisch Ostrau, 1923

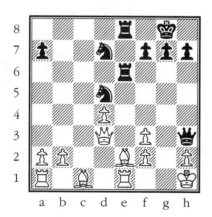

Solution: 21...Rxe2!

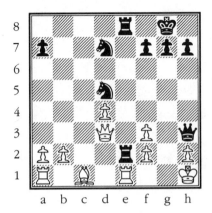

White resigned, because the rook cannot leave the first rank without allowing ...Qf1#. 22.Bd2. 22.Rd1 Re1+ 22...Nf4! and mate comes at g2 or on the back rank.

CAPABLANCA VS. JANOWSKI
New York, 1924

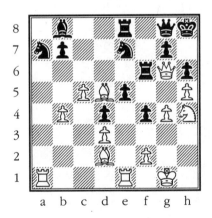

Solution: 39.Qxf6!

39.Bxg8 Nxg6; 40.Nxg6+ Kxg8 is also good for White, who can take advantage of the overworked bishop at b8 by 41.Nxe5 but 41...Rxe5; 42.Rxe5 Bxe5; 43.Rxa7 Rf7 is not over by any means.

39...gxf6; 40.Bxg8 Rxg8.

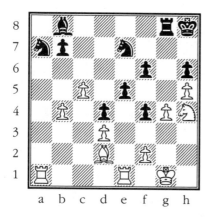

This is a more efficient path, because Black is saddled with a terrible bishop at b8 and the seemingly strong pawn at e5 is actually vulnerable to **41.f3 f5; 42.Bxf4!** The pin on the e-file adds to Black's woes.

42...Nec6; 43.Ng6+ Kh7; 44.Bxe5 Nxe5; 45.Rxe5 Bxe5; 46.Rxa7. Black resigned. The attacks at b7 and e5 are just too much.

KUPCHIK VS. CAPABLANCA
Lake Hopaton, 1926

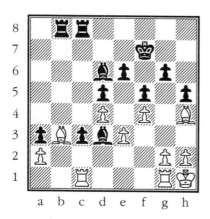

Solution: 38...Rxb3!; 39.axb3 a2.

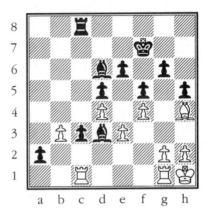

White resigned. The threat of the interference ...Bb1 forces the White rook to sit in the corner. 40.Ra1. 40.Be1 Bb1; 41.Bxc3 Rxc3!; 42.Rxb1 (42.Rxc3 a1Q) 42...axb1Q; 43.Rxb1 Rxe3 is not worth continuing. 40...Bb1; 41.Be1. Something must be done about that c-pawn. 41...c2; 42.Bd2. The c1–square is under control, for a moment. 42...Ba3!; 43.Bc1 Bxc1; 44.Rxc1 Rc3. White's rooks are paralyzed. 45.Kg1 Rd3; 46.Kf2 Rd1 wins.

A most amusing final position!

RETI VS. CAPABLANCA
Berlin, 1928

Solution: 15...0–0–0.

Black is willing to give back a little material to take the initiative. After White takes the rook Black will have his queen bishop, knight, queen and rook all aiming at White's king, which has no defenders. **16.Bxh8.**

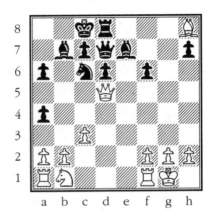

16...Ne5. Now White's queen won't be able to get back to defend the kingside.

17.Qd1. 17.Qd4 is suicide. 17...Nf3+!; 18.gxf3 (18.Kh1 Nxd4) 18...Rg8+; 19.Qg4 Qxg4+; 20.fxg4 Rxg4#. **17...Bf3.** Anything to open the g-file! **18.gxf3 Qh3.** White has no defense to threats like 19...Nxf3+ and 19...Rg8+, so Reti gave up.

STAHLBERG VS. ALEKHINE
Hamburg Olympiad, 1930

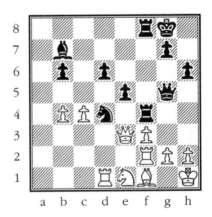

Solution: 31...Rxf3!!

White resigned. 32.Rxf3 Qxe3 costs White the queen because 33.Rxe3 allows 33...Rxf1# while 32.gxf3 drops the queen directly. If 32...Qxe3; 32.Qxg5 Rxf2; 33.Nf3 Bxf3 cleans up. 32.Qxf3 also fails: 32...Nxf3; 33.Nxf3 Qe3 with a pin on the f-file that can be exploited by advancing the e-pawn, and in any case Black's material advantage is decisive.

NAEGELI VS. EUWE
Bern, 1932

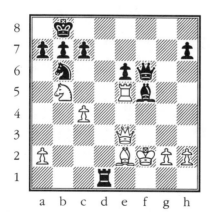

Solution: 31...Be4+!

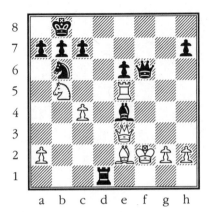

The discovered check doubles as an interference! White resigned, faced with the inevitable loss of material. 32.Kg3 Qxe5+ wins the rook.

BOTVINNIK VS. SPIELMANN
Moscow, 1935

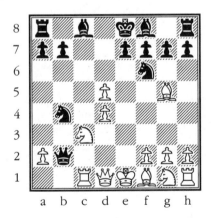

Trap the enemy queen!

Solution: 9.Na4.

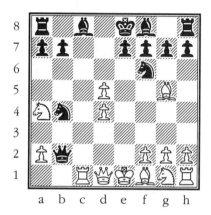

9...Qxa2. 9...Qa3; 10.Rc3 Qxa2 is similarly refuted by 11.Bc4. **10.Bc4 Bg4.** 10...Qa3; 11.Rc3! (11.Ra1?? would be a blunder because of the fork 11...Nc2+ and the knight cannot be captured because the rook is loose.) 11...Bg4; 12.Rxa3 Bxd1; 13.Bb5+ Nd7; 14.Kxd1 with an extra piece for White.
11.Nf3 Bxf3; 12.gxf3.

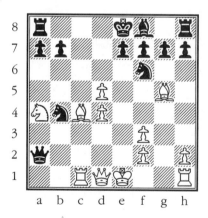

Black resigned. The queen is trapped and can only be liberated by 12...Nc2+ but despite the shattered pawns, the position after 13.Qxc2 Qxc2; 14.Rxc2 is hopeless for Black.

LASKER VS. LEVENFISH
Moscow, 1936

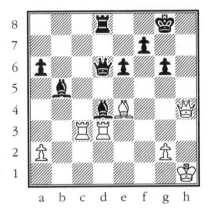

Solution: 34.Bxg6!

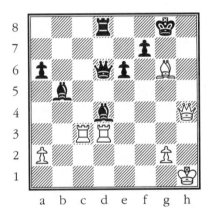

The computers prefer the retreat of the rook. **34.Rd2 Bxc3!** allows an x-ray blast at d8, but **35.Qxd8+ Qxd8; 36.Rxd8+ Kg7** is better for Black, because White has no targets and Black can use the bishop pair effectively and advance the pawns.

34...fxg6; 35.Rh3. A rook is offered at c3, but Black cannot bite. **35...Qd7.** 35...Bxc3??; 36.Qh7+ Kf8; 37.Rf3+ Ke8; 38.Qf7# is too simple. **36.Rcg3.**

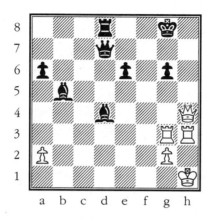

Black threatens ...Bd5 and ...Qd1+. **36...Bd3.** Not best, but the alternatives also lose:

36...Be5 sets up the back rank check. 37.Rxg6+ checkmates first. 37...Kf7; 38.Qh7+ Kf8; 39.Rg8#. 36...Qf7; 37.Qxd8+ and the bishop at d4 falls, protecting g1, if White doesn't checkmate or win the enemy queen.

36...Qe8; 37.Qh7+ Kf8; 38.Rf3+ and Black's army is forced to fall on their swords with 38...Bf6; 39.Rxf6+ Qf7; 40.Qxf7#.

36...Bg7; 37.Qh7+ Kf8; 38.Rf3+ Ke7; 39.Qxg7+ Kd6; 40.Rf7 wraps it up quickly, for example 40...Qc6; 41.Qd4+ Qd5; 42.Qb6+ forking the king and rook. 42...Ke5 is the only way to save the rook, but it drops the queen to 43.Re3+ Qe4; 44.Rxe4+ Kxe4; 45.Qxd8 and mate follows before long. 36...Rf8; 37.Rxg6+ Bg7; 38.Qh7+ Kf7; 39.Rxg7+ wins.

37.Rxd3.

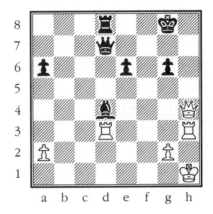

Black resigned. Even Black's best defense fails to a cute tactic. 37...Kf8; 38.Qxd8+! Qxd8; 39.Rh8+! The bishop at d4 is pinned, and cannot intervene. In the endgame it will be free, but no match for the rook with all of the poor pawns sitting on light squares. 39...Bxh8; 40.Rxd8+ Kg7; 41.Ra8!; 41.Re8 a5!; 42.Rxe6 Kf7; 43.Ra6 Bc3 is much more difficult. 41...g5; 42.Rxa6 Kf7; 43.a4 Ke7; 44.a5 Kd7; 45.Ra8 Bd4; 46.a6 Kc7; 47.Re8 Kd7; 48.Rg8 wins the g-pawn and the rest is simple. Black cannot play 48...Be3 because the bishop is overworked. The most efficient win is 49.a7! forcing 49...Bxa7; 50.Rg7+ and the bishop goes.

EUWE VS. TARTAKOWER
Nottingham, 1936

Solution: 21.e5!

The double attack at b7 and f7 is already on the board, and now the knight and f-pawn are under assault. Moreover, there is the threat of the pawn reaching e6. It must be eliminated! **21...fxe5; 22.Nxe5.** The fork at d7 leads to the win of material. **22...Qxe7; 23.Nxf7 Nxf7; 24.Qxb7.** The pawn which was under attack drops, and then the seventh rank becomes a killing ground. **24...Rd8; 25.Rxc7.**

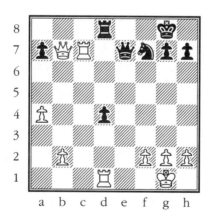

Black's resignation would have been justified here.
25...Qe6; 26.Re7 Qf6; 27.Qd7! Rf8. 27...Rxd7 gets checkmated by **28.Re8#. 28.Re8 Nd6; 29.Rxf8+ Kxf8; 30.Rd3 Qe5; 31.Kf1 h5; 32.Qxa7** and White won without difficulty.

ALEKHINE VS. RESHEVSKY
Kemeri, 1937

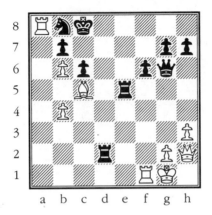

Solution: 35.Rxb8+!

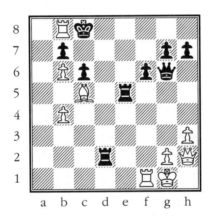

The king is drawn to b8, where it is vulnerable to a back rank mate. **35...Kxb8; 36.Qxe5+!!** Reshevsky resigned, because of 36...fxe5; 37.Rf8+ and mate follows.

BOTVINNIK VS. CAPABLANCA
Rotterdam, 1938

Solution: 34.Qf7+.
34.e7 was Botvinnik's choice.

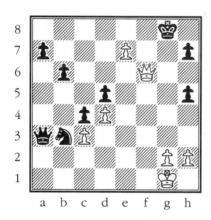

The best plan is 34.Qf7+ Kh8; 35.g3! Botvinnik considered only Baum's recommendation of advancing the pawn to e7, but that leads to perpetual check. (35.e7 Qc1+; 36.Kf2 Qd2+; 37.Kg3 Qg5+; 38.Kf3 Nd2+; 39.Ke2 Qg4+!; 40.Kxd2 Qxg2+; 41.Kc1 Qg1+; 42.Kb2 Qxh2+; 43.Ka3 Qd6+; 44.Ka4 Qc6+; 45.Ka3 Qd6+; 46.Kb2 Qh2+ etc.) 35...Nxd4 (35...Nd2; 36.e7 Nf3+ is similar.) 36.e7 Nf3+; 37.Kf2 Qb2+; 38.Kxf3 Qxc3+; 39.Kg2 Qd2+; 40.Kh3 and there are no more checks. So it is mate in two, beating Botvinnik's line by four moves. Of course any clear win is fine!

34...Qc1+; 35.Kf2 Qc2+; 36.Kg3 Qd3+; 37.Kh4 Qe4+; 38.Kxh5 Qe2+; 39.Kh4 Qe4+ (39...Qe1+; 40.g3 Qe4+; 41.g4 transposes); **40.g4 Qe1+; 41.Kh5.** White resigned, since it is mate in six: 41...h6; 42.Qg6+ Kh8; 43.e8Q+ Qxe8; 44.Qxe8+ Kg7; 45.Qe7+ Kg8; 46.Kg6.

ALEKHINE VS. KIENINGER
Poland, 1941

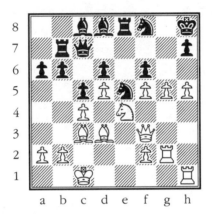

Solution: 25.gxf6!!

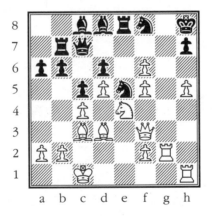

The bishop at c3 is just dying for the knight to get out of the way and enable a discovered check.

25...Qf7. If Black had captured the queen, a nasty surprise would have been sprung by Alekhine: 25...Nxf3; 26.f7+ Ne5; 27.Rg8#. **26.Rhg1!!**

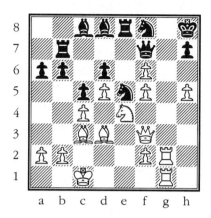

The queen is still taboo. **26...h6.** 26...Nxf3 leads to an ignominious fate. 27.Rg8+ Qxg8; 28.f7+ Qg7; 29.Bxg7#. **27.Bxe5 Rxe5; 28.Rg7.**

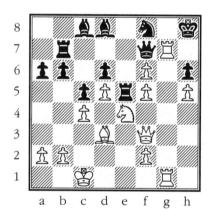

The Black queen is the first to leave the board, because she cannot retreat without yielding control of g8.

28...Qxg7. 28...Qe8; 29.Rg8+ Kh7; 30.Qg4 Qf7; 31.Rg7+ etc. **29.fxg7+ Rxg7; 30.Rxg7 Kxg7; 31.f6+.** Black resigned. 31...Kh8; 32.Nxd6 attacks the bishop and threatens a fork at f7.

BOTVINNIK VS. RAGOZIN
Leningrad (match), 1940

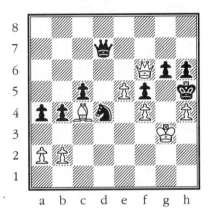

Solution: 57.e6!

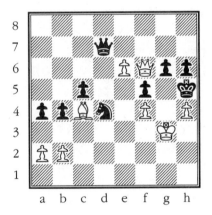

The advanced pawn is danger enough, but White also threatens to capture the knight with the queen and then deliver mate at e2. Black resigned.

ALEKHINE VS. RETHY
Munich, 1941

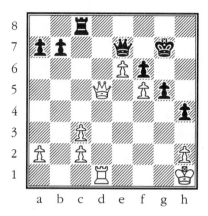

Solution: 30.Qd7!

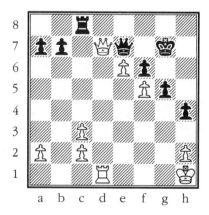

The Black queen is pinned, and there is a double attack at e7 and c8. **30...Re8.** 30...Rc7 loses to 31.Qxc7 Qxc7; 32.Rd7+! Qxd7; 33.exd7 with a new queen. **31.Qa4!** The d7 square is made available to the rook.

31...Rd8; 32.Rxd8. Black resigned. 32...Qxd8; 33.Qd7+ Qxd7; 34.exd7 is the same bad news.

DENKER VS. BOTVINNIK
Match (USA vs. USSR), 1945

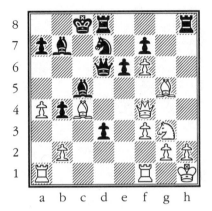

Solution: 22...Rxh2+!!

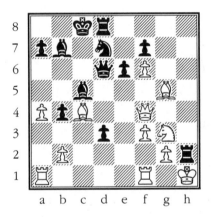

23.Kxh2 Rh8+; 24.Qh4. 24.Bh4 drops the queen to 24...Qxf4.
24...Rxh4+; 25.Bxh4 Qf4. The bishop is trapped, so White resigned.

SMYSLOV VS. KAMYSHOV
Moscow City Championship, 1945

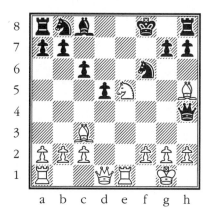

Solution: 15.Bg6!

15...Na6. Obviously the bishop could not be captured because White would recapture with the knight, setting up a family fork. 15...Bh3 is a clever reply. 16.gxh3 Qg5+ seems to buy time to grab the bishop at g6, but 17.Qg4! is the incredible reply. 17...Nxg4 (17...Qxg4+; 18.hxg4 hxg6; 19.Nxg6+ Kg8; 20.Bxf6 gxf6; 21.Re8+ Kg7; 22.Nxh8 wins.) 18.Bb4+! The win comes from a surprising queenside maneuver. 18...Qe7; 19.Nxg4 and Black cannot even take the bishop at b4 because of mate at e8. **16.Qe2.**

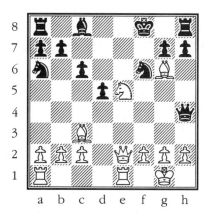

The mating plan is to move the knight and then sacrifice the queen at e8 to create a mating net.

16...Bh3; 17.Nf3! Black resigned because Black cannot save the queen and stop White from playing Qe7+ at the same time.

PETROSIAN VS. KOROLKOV
Tbilisi, 1945

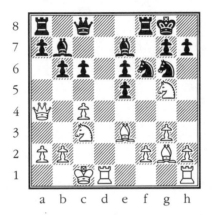

Solution: 15.Bh3!

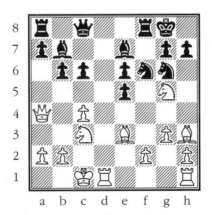

The e-pawn is lost.

15...Qe8; 16.Nxe6 b5; 17.Qb3. Now Black simply blunders a piece, overlooking the pin, but it hardly matters, since the rook at f8 could be taken at will. **17...bxc4; 18.Qxb7** and White won.

SMYSLOV VS. RUDAKOWSKY
Soviet Championship, 1945

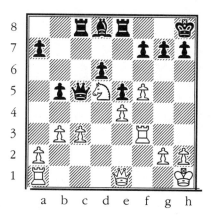

Solution: 22.f6!

The barriers start to fall.

22...gxf6; 23.Qh4! This was made possible by blocking the diagonal at f6. **23...Rg8; 24.Nxf6.** A little fork at h7 and g8, but Black cannot afford to capture the invader. **24...Rg7.** 24...Bxf6; 25.Qxf6+ Rg7; 26.Rg3 Rcg8; 27.Rd1 Qa3; 28.h4! Black is powerless against the advancing h-pawn.

25.Rg3 Bxf6; 26.Qxf6. Black resigned. White will bring the rook at a1, which has not yet moved, into the game with devastating effect. 26...Rcg8; 27.Rd1 Qa3; 28.h4 reaches the same position as the previous note.

SPASSKY VS. AFTONOV
Leningrad, 1949

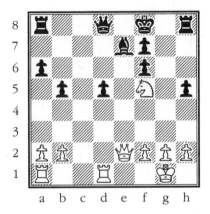

Solution: 19.Rxd5!

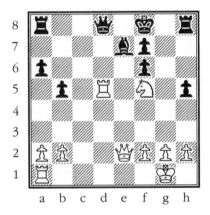

The overworked Black queen is deftly exploited to bring a rapid conclusion to the game. **19...Qxd5; 20.Qxe7+ Kg8; 21.Qxf6.** Mate at g7 or a fork at e7. Resignation was indeed the best choice.

BOTVINNIK VS. SMYSLOV
World Championship, 1954

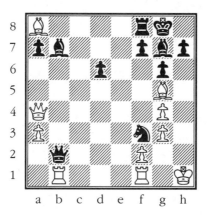

Solution: 22...Bxa8!

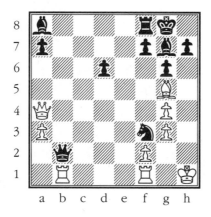

Smyslov parts with the queen, but keeps the option of discovered check.

23.Rxb2 Nxg5+; 24.Kh2 Nf3+! The knight returns to re-establish the discovered check. **25.Kh3 Bxb2; 26.Qxa7 Be4.**

Black's three minor pieces are more than a match for the king. If anything goes wrong, the position can be drawn by checking with the knight. **27.a4 Kg7; 28.Rd1 Be5; 29.Qe7 Rc8; 30.a5 Rc2.** Everybody gets into the act! **31.Kg2 Nd4+; 32.Kf1.**

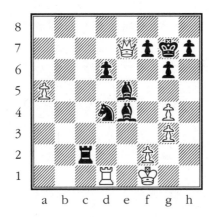

The king tries to get out of the box, but that's not going to happen.

32...Bf3; 33.Rb1 Nc6. Faced with the fork on the queen and the a-pawn, White gave up. The Black forces close in quickly, and the pawn at f2 is sure to fall. 34.Qc7 Bd4; 35.Qxd6 Rxf2+; 36.Ke1 Re2+; 37.Kf1 Rh2 leads to the win of the remaining White forces.

EUWE VS. FISCHER
New York, 1957

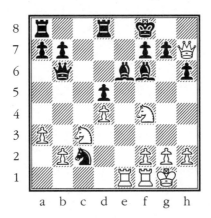

Solution: 19.Ncxd5.

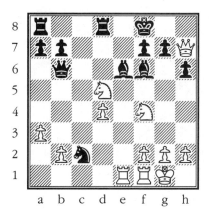

The knight at d5 chokes the e7 square, and Qh8# is available.
19...Rxd5; 20.Nxd5. Black resigned. If the knight is captured then Qh8 is checkmate.

TAL VS. KLIAVINS
Latvian Teams Championship, 1958

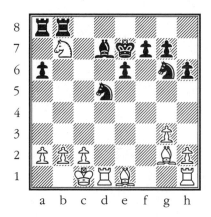

Solution: 22.Rxd5!

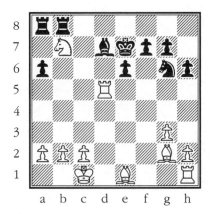

To Tal, such sacrifices were almost child's play. Actually, it is hardly a sacrificed since Black can't take either piece.

22...Bc6. The best practical chance. 22...Rxb7? would lose to 23.Rxd7+ Rxd7; 24.Bxa8 with an extra piece. 22...exd5; 23.Bb4+ forces 23...Ke8; 24.Re1+ Be6 when 25.Bxd5 is deadly, threatening discovered check with Nd6+.

23.Bb4+ Ke8; 24.Rd8+ Rxd8; 25.Bxc6+. Black resigned.

TAL VS. NEI
Soviet Union, 1958

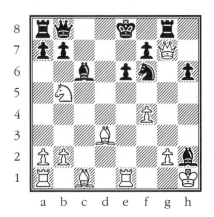

Solution: 19.Rxe6+!!

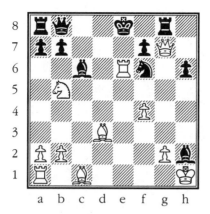

The pawn at f7 must give way.

    19...fxe6. 19...Kd7; 20.Qxf7+ Kd8; 21.Qxf6+ Kc8; 22.Bf5 Bd7; 23.Re7 wins.

    20.Bg6+ Kd8; 21.Qxf6+. Black resigned. The end is near. 21...Kd7; 22.Qf7+ Kd8; 23.Qxg8+ Kd7; 24.Qf7+ Kd8; 25.Qf8+ Kd7; 26.Be8+! Qxe8; 27.Qd6+ Kc8; 28.Qc7#.

NIEMALA VS. SPASSKY
Riga, 1959

Solution: 34...Rb8!!

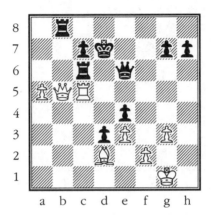

The queen has to guard the rook at c5.

35.Rd5+. 35.Qxb8 Rxc5; 36.Bb4 Rc1+; 37.Kg2 Qf5 wins quickly.
35...Kc8; 36.Rd8+. White uses a deflection to maintain the initiative, but that is all he can accomplish. **36...Kxd8; 37.Qxb8+ Kd7; 38.Qb5 Kc8; 39.Kg2 Rd6.** White is lost now.

40.Qb2 Qf7; 41.Qe5 Qf3+; 42.Kg1 Qd1+; 43.Kg2 Qxd2. Black won.

PETROSIAN VS. NIELSEN
Copenhagen, 1960

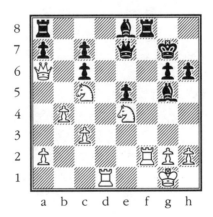

Solution: 23.Rxf8!

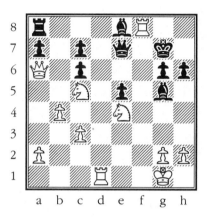

This brings the king to f8. **23...Kxf8.** 23...Qxf8 drops the queen to the fork 24.Ne6+. **24.Nxg5 hxg5.**

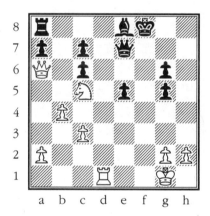

Black's extra pawn is a joke, and White now delivers the final blow. 24...Qxg5; 25.Ne6+ is a variation on the same theme.

25.Qb7 and Black resigned. The rook has no escape: 25...Rd8; 26.Rxd8 Qxd8; 27.Ne6+.

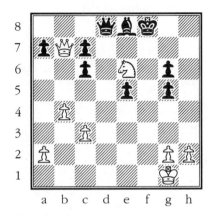

Finally, the fork is achieved.

UNZICKER VS. TAL
W. Germany vs. Soviet Union Hamburg, 1960

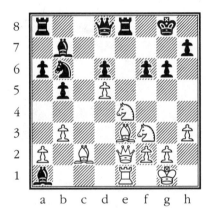

Solution: 23...Nxd5!; 24.Rxa1 Nxe3!

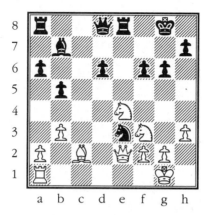

25.Qxe3. White must take with the queen or else the interference at e3 will leave the knight at e4 defenseless. **25...Bxe4; 26.Bxe4 d5.** White resigned, since the bishop is lost. 27.Rd1 Rxe4; 28.Qxe4 dxe4; 29.Rxd8+ Rxd8 etc.

LETELIER VS. FISCHER
Leipzig Olympiad, 1960

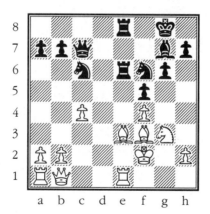

Solution: 21...Rxe3!; 22.Rxe3 Rxe3; 23.Kxe3.

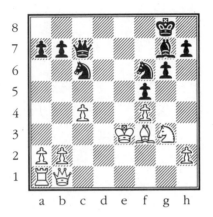

23...Qxf4+!! White resigned, because of the following finish.
24.Kf2. 24.Kxf4?? Bh6# mate. 24...Ng4+; 25.Kg2. 25.Ke2?? Qe3+;
26.Kd1 Nf2+; 27.Kc2 Nd4# mate. 25...Ne3+; 26.Kf2 Nd4; 27.Qh1
Ng4+; 28.Kf1 Nxf3 with more ugliness to follow.

NYEZHMETDINOV VS. TAL
Baku, 1961

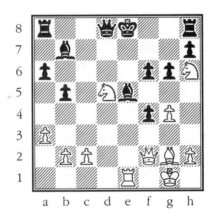

Solution: 23.Nxf6+!
The defender of the bishop falls.
23...Qxf6; 24.Qd4! The pin is exploited. **24...Kf8; 25.Rxe5.** A
discovered attack on the Black queen is threatened by Rf5.

25...Qd8. 25...Rd8; 26.Re8+!; **26.Rf5+.** Anyway! Now the discovery is on the rook at h8. **26...gxf5; 27.Qxh8+ Ke7**. The only move. **28.Qg7+ Ke6**. Or 28...Ke8; 29.Qf7#. **29.gxf5+.**

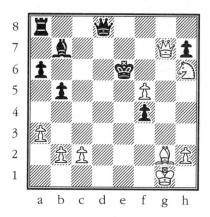

Black resigned because the king must go to either e5 or d6, and then Nf7+ forks king and queen.

PETROSIAN VS. PACHMAN
Bled, 1961

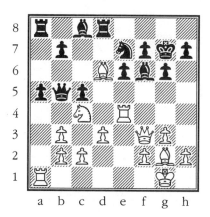

Solution: 19.Qxf6+!!

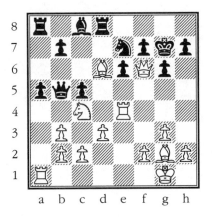

A fantastic sacrifice, one of Petrosian's best. The king is decoyed to f6. 19...Kxf6; 20.Be5+ Kg5. 20...Kf5; 21.Ne3+ Kg5; 22.Bg7 is similar. **21.Bg7.**

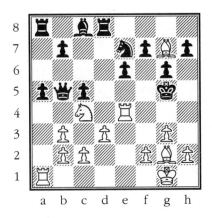

The Black king is doomed, so Pachman resigned. The conclusion might have been: 21...Nf5; 22.f4+ Kh5; 23.Bf3#.

TAL VS. BOTVINNIK
World Championship, 1961

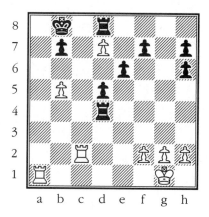

Solution: 31.Rc8+!

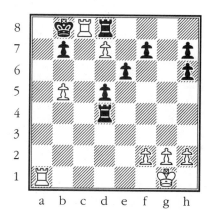

White brings the rook from d8 to c8. **31...Rxc8.** Now the king is deflected from b8. **32.Ra8+!!** Black resigned, because the pawn will promote.

TAL VS. GHITESCU
Miskolcz, 1963

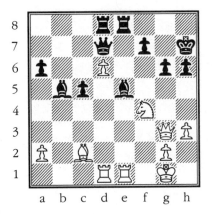

Solution: 35.Bxg6+!

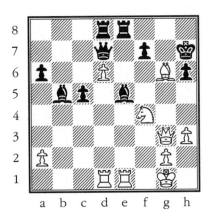

The bishop cannot be captured, and lives to offer his life again.
35...Kh8. 35...fxg6; 36.Qxg6+ Kh8; 37.Rxe5! Rxe5; 38.Qf6+ Qg7;
39.Qxd8+ Re8; 40.Qc7! with a winning position for White.

36.Bxf7! Bd4+. Interference on the d-file, but Tal sweeps it away.
36...Qxf7; 37.Ng6+ Kh7; 38.Nxe5. **37.Rxd4! Rxe1+; 38.Qxe1 Qxf7;**
39.Qe5+ Qg7; 40.Qxc5. Black resigned, lacking any serious
counterplay.

FISCHER VS. SUTTLES
United States Championship, 1965

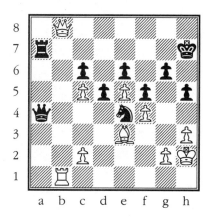

Solution: 33.Qf8!

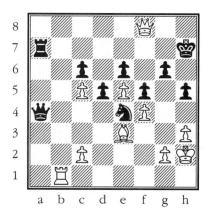

The Black king is trapped and the rook cannot defend against mate, but Black's queen and knight can't help. **33...Rg7; 34.Rb8.** Black cannot avoid mate in seven. **34...g5; 35.Qh8+ Kg6; 36.Qe8+ Rf7; 37.Rb7.** Black resigned. The longest defense is 37...Kh6; 38.Qxe6+ Nf6; 39.fxg5+ Kh7; 40.Qxf7+ Kh8; 41.Qg7#.

SPASSKY VS. LANGEWEG
Sochi, 1967

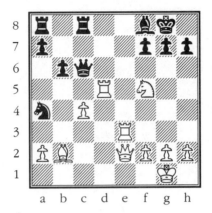

Solution: 25.Bxg7!

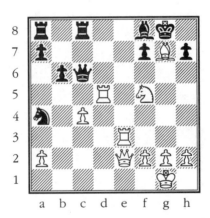

25...Qxd5!? 25...Qxc4; 26.Rg3! wins, for example 26...Bxg7; 27.Rxg7+ Kh8; 28.Qh5 Qc1+; 29.Rd1. **26.Nh6+! Kxg7; 27.Qg4+.** Black resigned. 27...Kh8; 28.Qg8# or 27...Kxh6; 28.Rh3+ and mate next move.

PETROSIAN VS. SPASSKY
World Championship, 1969

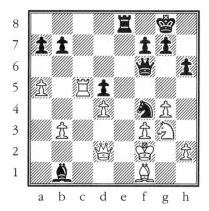

Solution: 38...Bd3!

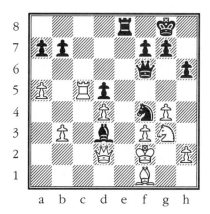

The pawn at d4 is under attack by the Black queen, who can take it with check and win the rook.

39.Nf5. 39.Bxd3 Qxd4+; 40.Kf1 Nxd3!; 41.Rc1. White takes advantage of the pin on the knight, but has no reply to 41...Re3! **39...Qg5** creates a new threat of discovered attack on the White queen.

40.Ne3 Qh4+; 41.Kg1 Bxf1. White resigned since he is mated after 42.Nxf1 Re2 while 42.Kxf1 is met by 42...Qh3+ and White must lose at least a piece.

LARSEN VS. TAL
Candidates Match, 1969

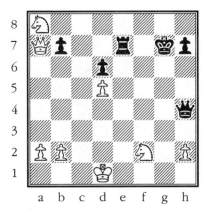

Solution: 35...Qc4!

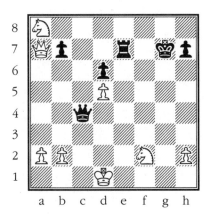

By taking away c2 and c1, the queen limits Black's exit to d2. In addition, White loses d4 as a checking square.

36.Qb6 Qf1+; 37.Kd2 Re2+. The knight is lost, but that is only a small part of the action. **38.Kc3 Qc1+; 39.Kd4 Qe3+; 40.Kc4 Rc2+** and Larsen resigned, since the king would have to move to the b-file, allowing ...Rxb2+ to win the queen at b6.

FISCHER VS. SCHWEBER
Buenos Aires, 1970

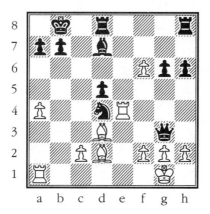

Solution: 24.Rxd4!!

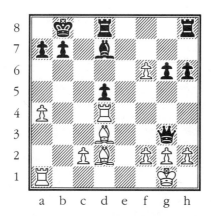

24...Qg4. Black had to offer the queen or else lose even more material. 24...Qc7 runs into the pin 25.Bf4, while 24...Qxd3; 25.Bf4+ Ka8; 26.cxd3 is a winning endgame, for example 26...Bf5; 27.Rc1 Rd7 (27...Rh7; 28.Rc7 Rxc7; 29.Bxc7 Re8; 30.g4! Be6; 31.h4 and White hangs on to the extra pawn.) 28.Bxh6! The back rank is too weak.

25.Rxg4 Bxg4; 26.Bxg6.

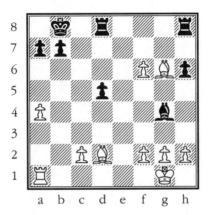

White has a bishop and two pawns for the exchange, and the pawn at f6 is far advanced. The game continued **26...Rhg8; 27.Bh7 Rh8; 28.Bd3 Rde8; 29.f7 Re7; 30.f8Q+ Rxf8; 31.Bb4 Rff7; 32.Bxe7 Rxe7; 33.f3** and the rest was easy. White won.

ALBURT VS. TAL
Soviet Championship, 1972

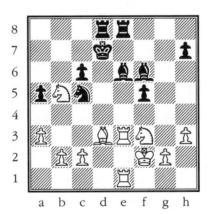

Solution: 23...f4!

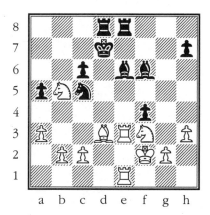

The rook is driven from e3, so that the bishop can be captured with check without allowing White to respond in kind.

24.Re5. 24.R3e2 Nxd3+; 25.cxd3 cxb5 is no better. **24...Nxd3+; 25.cxd3 cxb5; 26.Rxb5 Rb8**. White has not got enough pawns for the piece. **27.Ne5+ Kd6; 28.Rxa5? Bh4+**. The x-ray at e1 caused White to resign.

TAL VS. CASTRO
Interzonal Biel, 1976

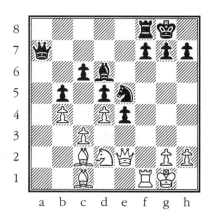

Solution: 23.Nxe4! dxe4; 24.Qxe4.

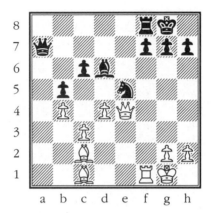

White has returned the piece and material is, for the moment, equal. The simultaneous attack on a7 and c6 proves decisive.

24...Ng6. 24...g6 is pierced by a sharp pin. 25.Bf4! **25.Qxc6.** Another double attack, at b5 and d6. **25...Qb8; 26.h3 Ne7; 27.Qe4 g6.** 27...Ng6; 28.Qf5 immobilizes Black.

28.Qf3. Black resigned. The bishop will come to h6 and then the defender of f7 must flee.

PETROSIAN VS. ALBURT
Soviet Championship, 1977

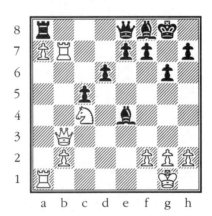

Solution: 34.Rb8!

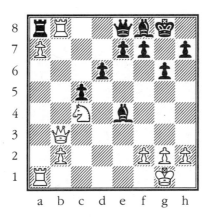

34...Qd7. 34...Rxb8; 35.axb8Q is pointless. **35.Rxa8 Bxa8; 36.Nb6.**

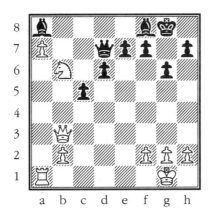

Finally the hammer blow is delivered. **36...Qb7.** One last hope—the mate at g2. **37.Qf3.** Black resigned. 37...Qxf3; 38.gxf3 Bc6; 39.a8Q Bxa8; 40.Rxa8 wins.

SIBAREVIC VS. KASPAROV
Banja Luka, 1979

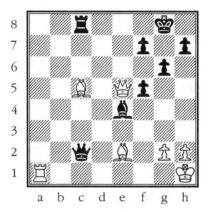

Solution: 32...Qxe2!

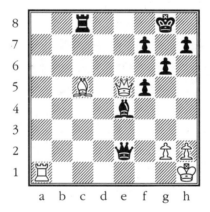

White resigned, because there is a threatened mate at g2. 33.Qg3. 33.Rg1 Bxg2+ is a discovered attack that wins the queen. 33...Rxc5 wins the bishop.

KASPAROV VS. LIGTERINK
Malta Olympiad, 1980

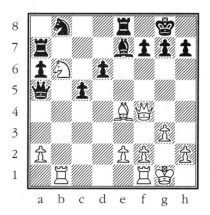

Solution: 22.Nc8!

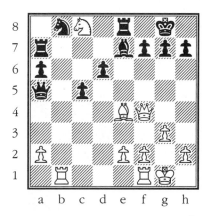

White forks three Black pieces, the point being that the capture allows a fork with a mating threat. **22...Nc6.** 22...Rxc8 loses to 23.Qf5 when the threat is Qxh7+ and Qh8#, so the rook at c8 falls, and the knight at b8 as well.

22...Rc7; 23.Rxb8 Bf8 is a last desperate attempt to save the game but it does not succeed. (23...Rcxc8; 24.Rxc8 Rxc8; 25.Qf5 as in the previous note.) 24.Nxd6! White ignores the pin. 24...Rxb8; 25.Nc4 wins a rook.

23.Nxa7 Nxa7; 24.Bd5. Black resigned. The threat at f7 forces Black to choose between three inadequate defenses. 24...Rf8. 24...Qc7; 25.Qxf7+ Kh8; 26.Qxe8+ mates. 24...Bf6; 25.Rb7 Nb5; 26.Bxf7+ Kf8; 27.Bxe8 Kxe8; 28.Qe4+ wins. 25.Rb7 Nc8; 26.Rfb1 followed by Rb8 and R1b7 is not worth playing, even in an Olympiad.

KASPAROV VS. KUIJPERS
Dortmund, 1980

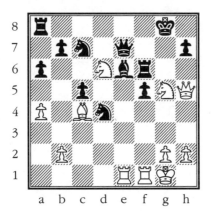

Solution: 24.Nxf5.

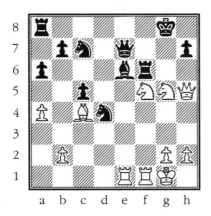

Obvious enough. But after **24...Nxf5** you need to capture with the correct piece.

25.Nxe6. White threatens to wipe out the enemy army with Nxc7+, a discovered check which wins all of Black's pieces. **25...Nxe6.**

26.Rxe6 Rxe6. Again, no choice because of the discovered check threats. **27.Qxf5!** There is no rush to capture the rook. Kasparov just piles up on the pinned piece. **27...Re8; 28.Re1.** Black resigned, because the rook at e6 is lost.

KARPOV VS. ALBURT
Malta Olympiad, 1980

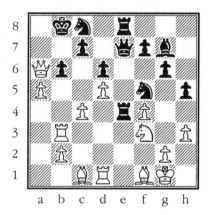

27.c5!

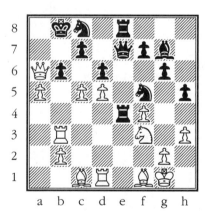

The pressure at d6 proves deadly. The clearance allows White to make more threats, and the barrier collapses in a few moves.

27...dxc5; 28.Bb5! The light squares provide all the illumination needed for victory. **28...c6; 29.Bxc6.**

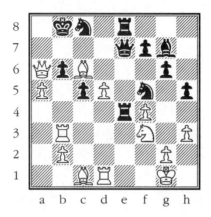

There is danger in the corner, and a simple defense does not exist.

29...Bd4+. 29...Qa7; 30.Qxa7+ Kxa7 (30...Nxa7; 31.Rxb6+ Kc8; 32.Bxe8 Rxe8; 33.d6 wins.) 31.axb6+ Nxb6; 32.Bd2! The path is cleared for the rook at d1 to get to the a-file, and the bishop can be useful later at a5. 32...R8e7; 33.Ra1+ Kb8; 34.Rxb6+ Kc7; 35.Rb7+ Kd6; 36.Rb8! Black may as well resign, a piece down with a nasty check looming at d8.

30.Nxd4 Nxd4; 31.axb6. Black can only delay the inevitable, and after **31...Nf3+; 32.Rxf3 Re1+; 33.Rxe1** Alburt resigned.

KAVALEK VS. KASPAROV
Bugojno, 1982

Solution: 27...Nc1.

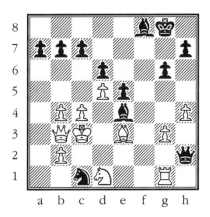

White resigned, despite a material advantage. The fork applies to the queen at b3, and the e2-square, which checks the king and attacks the rook at g1. 28.Qa4. 28.Bxc1 drops the rook immediately to 28...Qxg1 and even though material is almost even, White can't defend the king. 29.Be3 Qe1+; 30.Bd2 Qe2 threatens Qd3#, and the Black king has no room to run. 28...Ne2+; 29.Kb3 Nxg1; 30.Bxg1 Bc2+. Intermezzo! 31.Ka3 Bxa4; 32.Bxh2 Bxd1 and there is no reason to continue.

TIMMAN VS. KASPAROV
Bugojno, 1982

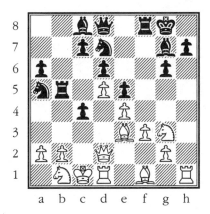

Solution: 16.b4.

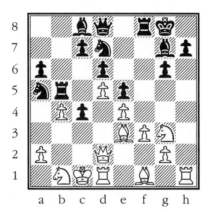

If the knight retreats, the rook has nowhere to go when attacked by the a-pawn.

16...cxb3; 17.Bxb5. Black can't even take the bishop, because then the knight at a5 falls. **17...c5.** This saves the knight, which is now protected by the queen. The pawn at b3 is safe because of the threatened fork, and there is an attack at a2, so the game is not yet clear. **18.dxc6.** Now the knight at d7 is under assault. **18...axb5.**

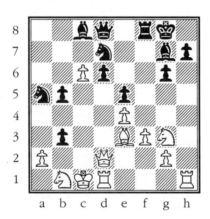

White should be winning easily here, but Timman fails to make the most of his chances. 19.Qd5+; 19.cxd7 Nc4; 20.dxc8Q Qxc8; 21.axb3? Nxd2+; 22.Kxd2! would have given White a rook and two knights for queen and pawn in a position where the king could easily be kept safe from harm.

19...Rf7. 19...Kh8 would have run into a familiar checkmating pattern. 20.Rxh7+ Kxh7; 21.Rh1+ Bh6; 22.Bxh6. **20.axb3 Nf8; 21.Qxd6 Qe8.** White should play Kb2 to secure the king, but instead tries to find some way to win the game via direct attack. After all, he is up the exchange and two pawns, though one is being returned immediately. Instead, Timman allowed Kasparov to get back into the game, which was eventually drawn.

ALBURT VS. KASPAROV
Lucerne Olympiad 1982

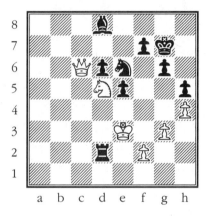

Solution: 51...Re2+!

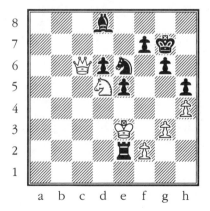

52.Kd3. The rook cannot be captured because of 52...Nd4+, forking the king and queen. **52...e4+; 53.Kc4.** 53.Kc3 Rc2+!!; 54.Kxc2

Nd4+ achieves the fork.

53...Rc2+; 54.Nc3. Black has blocked the check but the knight gets pinned. **54...Bf6; 55.Qxe4 Rxc3+; 56.Kd5 Rc5+!; 57.Kxd6 Be5+.** White resigned. 58.Qxe5+ Rxe5; 59.Kxe5 leaves Black a piece down. 58.Kd7 is met by 58...Rc7+; 59.Ke8 Bd6 and the threat of ...Re7 mate is unstoppable.

NIKOLIC VS. KASPAROV
Niksic, 1983

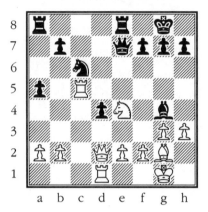

Solution: 20...Bxe2!

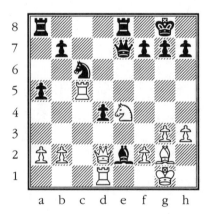

21.Re1. 21.Qxe2 drops the exchange to 21...Qxc5 but the position remains a little complicated after 22.Nxc5 Rxe2; 23.Nxb7. Still, with 23...Nd8; 24.Rxd4 Nxb7; 25.Bxb7 Rb8, White wins one of the queenside pawns and should win.

21...d3. The bishop is secured and Black has a clear advantage. The game continued **22.Qc3 Rad8; 23.Nd2 Nd4; 24.Qxa5 h6; 25.Rc3 b6; 26.Qa6 Qg5; 27.Rxd3 Qg6; 28.Bf1 Qxd3; 29.Qxd3 Bxd3; 30.Rxe8+ Rxe8; 31.Bxd3 Re1+; 32.Bf1 Ra1; 33.Nc4 b5; 34.Nd6 Rxa2; 35.Nxb5 Nxb5; 36.Bxb5 Rxb2.**

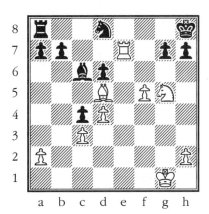

Black is up a clear exchange. It took a long time, but Kasparov eventually won.

KASPAROV VS. IVANCHUK
Soviet Championship, 1988

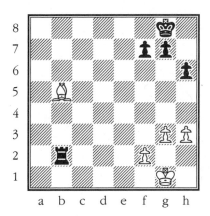

Solution: 24.f6!

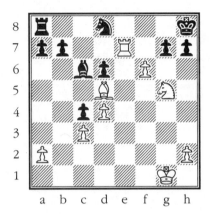

Black resigned. White threatens fxg7#, and the bishop at c6 cannot capture at d5 because of the back rank mate at e8.

KARPOV VS. MALANIUK
Soviet Championship, 1988

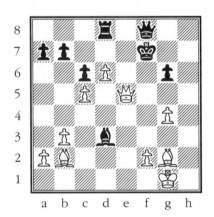

Solution: 35.Bd5+!!

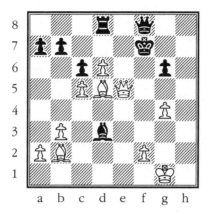

35...cxd5; 36.Qxd5+ Ke8; 37.Qe6+ Qe7; 38.Qxe7#.

SMYSLOV VS. BLACKSTOCK
London (Lloyds Bank), 1988

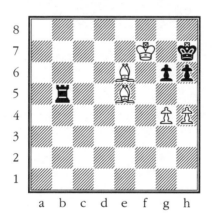

Solution: 62.h5!

Black resigned, for if the g-pawn moves, Bf5+ is mate. The only try is a check, but it bounces. 62...Rb7+; 63.Kf8 Rb6. The White bishop prevents a check at b8. Mate is unavoidable. 63...gxh5; 64.Bf5#. 63...g5; 64.Bf5#; 64.Bg8#.

KARPOV VS. NIKOLIC
Skelleftea, 1989

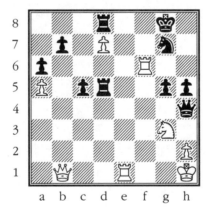

Solution: 43.Re8+.

This is a killer diversion. Black resigned on the spot, because of 43...Rxe8; 44.dxe8Q+ Nxe8; 45.Qg6+ Ng7; 46.Qf7+ Kh7; 47.Qxd5. Or, equally unpleasant, 43...Nxe8; 44.dxe8Q+ Rxe8; 45.Qg6+ Kh8; 46.Qxe8+ Kg7; 47.Qf8+ Kh7; 48.Rh6#.

FISCHER VS. SPASSKY
Match, 1992

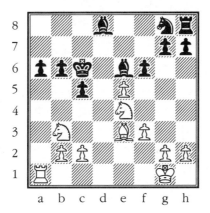

Solution: 19.Nbxc5!

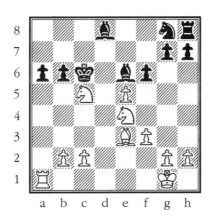

The barriers fall, and White wins by force.

19...Bc8. 19...bxc5; 20.Rxa6+ Kd7; 21.Nxc5+ Ke7; 22.Nxe6 g6; 23.Bc5+ Ke8; 24.Ra8 and White wins the bishop. **20.Nxa6 fxe5; 21.Nb4+.**

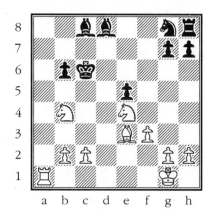

Black resigned. One of the bishops must fall. Let's consider all the legal replies. 21...Kc7. 21...Kb7; 22.Nd6+ Kc7; 23.Nf7 traps the rook at h8. 21...Kd7; 22.Rd1+ Kc7; 23.Bxb6+ Kxb6; 24.Rxd8 Bf5; 25.Nd5+ Ka7; 26.Nd6 is a very pretty position—for White! 21...Kb5; 22.Nd6+ Kxb4; 23.Ra3! The little rook lift covers b3 so that checkmate can be delivered by the c-pawn. 22.Ra7+ Bb7. (22...Kb8; 23.Nc6#); 23.Rxb7+! Kxb7; 24.Nd6+ Ka8; 25.Nf7 and the rook goes.

SPASSKY VS. FISCHER
Match, 1992

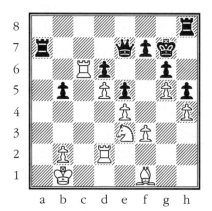

Solution: 37...Ra1+!!

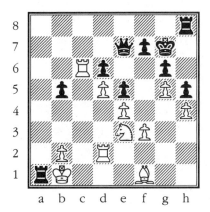

This tactic seems to just lose the exchange, but the threats just keep on coming. 37...Rb8 would win eventually, but the sacrifice is more efficient.

38.Kxa1 Qa7+; 39.Kb1 Qxe3. The queen attacks the rook and f-pawn, and also a triple attack with a check at e1. **40.Kc2 b4.** Spassky resigned. Loss of further material is inevitable. 41.Bd3 b3+; 42.Kc3 Ra8 and the rook can circle to c1. In any case, the pawns at f3 and h4 will be uprooted, and more devastation would follow.

CHABANON VS. KASPAROV
French Team Championship, 1993

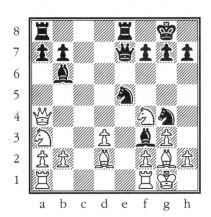

Solution: 21...Nxf2!

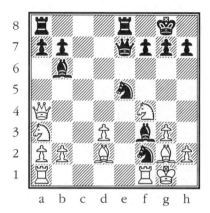

The demolition derby begins.
22.Rxf2 Bxg2; 23.Kxg2 Bxf2; 24.Kxf2.

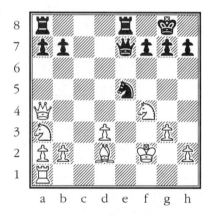

White has a bishop and knight for the rook, but the king is defended by two minor pieces, and they can't afford to move. 24...g5! If the knight moves, then the pawn at d3 falls with check and nasty consequences.

25.Qe4 gxf4; 26.gxf4 Qh4+. White resigned, facing a hopeless situation after 27.Kf1 Qh3+; 28.Qg2+. 28.Kg1 Nf3+; 29.Kf2 Rxe4; 30.dxe4 Nxd2 with an extra queen. 28.Ke2 Nxd3; 29.Rg1+ Kf8 wins the queen. 28...Qxg2+; 29.Kxg2 Nxd3 and more material will soon be lost.

KASPAROV VS. SHORT
Amsterdam (Euwe Memorial), 1994

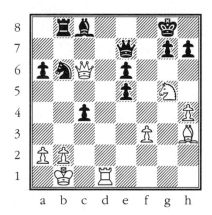

Solution: 28.Qe4.

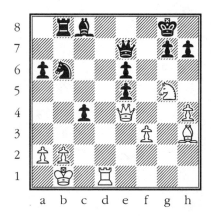

The threat at h7 is serious, so the pawn at e5 falls.

28...g6; 29.Qxe5. The weakling is pinned and will be gobbled up after the rook gets to d6. There is nothing Black can do about it.

29...Rb7; 30.Rd6 c3; 31.Bxe6+ Bxe6; 32.Rxe6. Black resigned. Kasparov provided the following convincing conclusion:

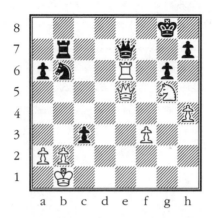

32...Nc4; 33.Qxc3 Na3+; 34.Kc1 Qd7; 35.Rc6 and the threat of Rc8+ is fatal.

KARPOV VS. GEORGIEV
Tilburg, 1994

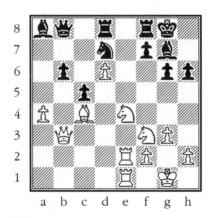

Solution: 29.Bxf7+!

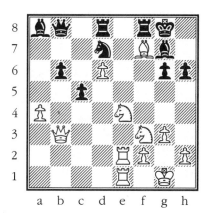

First the pawn at f7 is removed, and the capturing rook is pinned by the queen.

29...Rxf7; 30.Neg5!! A knight is sacrificed to get the other knight to g8, when the pin is excruciating. **30...hxg5; 31.Nxg5 Rdf8.**

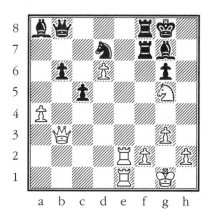

The rook is defended, but the rook at f8 can't defend both f7 and e8 for long.

32.Re8! Qxd6. Black's king is defended by almost all the pieces, and has two extra bishops. It isn't enough, because the rook at f8 is pinned, so f7 is not defended after all!; **33.Qxf7+ Kh8; 34.Ne6!** A final fork at f8 and g7 forced Black's resignation.

LAUTIER VS. KARPOV
Linares, 1995

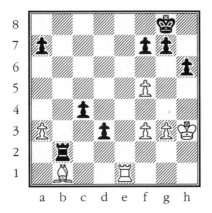

Solution: 40...Rxb1!

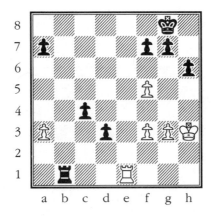

The exchange is sacrificed but the pawns march forward. White resigned. 41.Rxb1 c3; 42.Rd1 c2; 43.Rc1 d2 etc.

SOLUTIONS TO THE QUIZZES

DEEP BLUE VS. KASPAROV
Man vs. Machine, 1997

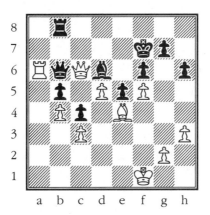

Solution: 45...Qe3!

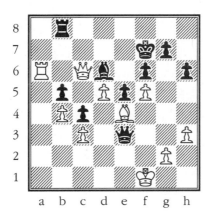

46.Qxd6. 46.Qd7+ Kg8; 47.Qxd6 Rf8; 48.Qe6+ Kh7; 49.Qe7 (49.Ra1 Qxe4; 50.d6 Qd3+; 51.Kg1 Qxc3 wins) 49...Rg8!; 50.Bf3 Qc1+; 51.Kf2 Qd2+; 52.Kg1 Qc1+; 53.Kf2 Qd2+; 54.Kg1 Qc1+; 55.Kh2 Qf4+; 56.Kg1 Qc1+; 57.Kf2 Qd2+ and White cannot escape the checks.

46...Re8; 47.Bf3. 47.Qc7+ Re7; 48.d6 Rxc7; 49.dxc7 Qf4+; 50.Kg1 Qc1+; 51.Kh2 Qf4+; 52.g3 Qxe4; 53.c8Q Qe2+ draws. 47.Qe6+ Rxe6; 48.fxe6+ Ke7; 49.Bg6 Qc1+; 50.Ke2 e4; 51.Bxe4 Qb2+; 52.Kf1 Qc1+; 53.Ke2 Qb2+; 54.Kf3 Qxc3+.

47.h4!? is the critical line. Black must now play 47...h5! After

48.Bf3 Qc1+; 49.Kf2 Qd2+; 50.Be2 Qf4+ the king cannot find shelter.
47.Qd7+ Re7; 48.Qxb5 Qxe4 is not a problem for Black.

47...Qc1+; 48.Kf2 Qd2+; 49.Be2. 49.Kg1 Qc1+; 50.Kh2 Qf4+;
51.g3 Qxf3; 52.Ra2 Qxf5; 53.Qc5 Qb1; 54.Ra7+ Kg8; 55.Qxb5 Qc2+;
56.Kg1 Qd1+ with perpetual check. **49...Qf4+; 50.Ke1 Qc1+; 51.Bd1
Qxc3+!; 52.Kf1 Qc1; 53.Ke2 Qb2+.**

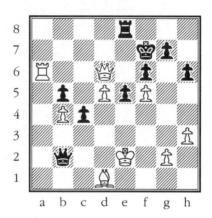

54.Ke1. 54.Kf3 loses to 54...Qc3+; 55.Kg4 Qe3!; 56.Qd7+ Re7;
57.Qxe7+ Kxe7 and White cannot hold on to the remaining pieces.
54...Qc3+; 55.Kf1 Qc1 with a draw.

RECOMMENDED READING

Alekhine, Alexander. *My Best Games*. Batsford.

Burger, Robert. *The Chess of Bobby Fischer*. Hypermodern Press.

Capablanca, Jose R. *Last Lectures*.

Divinksy, Nathan & Raymond Keene. *Warriors of the Mind*. Harding & Simpole.

Euwe, Max. *Strategy and Tactics in Chess*.

Euwe, Max. *From My Games*. Dover.

Fischer, Robert J. *My 60 Memorable Games*. Batsford.

Kasparov, Garry et. al. *Fighting Chess*. Batsford.

Keene, Raymond & Eric Schiller. *World Champion Combinations*. Cardoza.

Mednis, Edmar. *How Karpov Wins*. McKay.

Petrosian, Tigran. *Petrosian's Legacy*. Editions Erebouni.

Réti, Richard. *Masters of the Chessboard*. Dover.

Schiller, Eric. *The Big Book of Combinations*. Hypermodern Press.

Schiller, Eric. *World Champion Openings*. Cardoza.

Shamkovich, Leonid. *The Chess Terrorist's Handbook*. Hays.

Shamkovich, Leonid. *The Tactical World of Chess*. David McKay.

Shamkovich, Leonid & Jan Cartier. *Tactical Chess Training*. Hays.

Smyslov, Vasiy. *Endgame Virtuoso*. Cadogan.

Steinitz, Wilhelm. *Modern Chess Instructor*. Edition Olms.

CHESS PRODUCTS CATALOG

For the latest updated listings, go to our web site
www.cardozapub.com

CARDOZA PUBLISHING CHESS BOOKS

- OPENINGS -

WINNING CHESS OPENINGS by Bill Robertie - Shows concepts and best moves of more than 25 essential openings from Black and White perspectives: King's Gambit, Center Game, Scotch Game, Giuoco Piano, Vienna Game, Bishop's Opening, Ruy Lopez, French, Caro-Kann, Sicilian, Alekhine, Pirc, Modern, Queen's Gambit, Nimzo-Indian, Queen's Indian, Dutch, King's Indian, Benoni, English, Bird's, Reti's, and King's Indian Attack. Examples from 25 grandmasters and champions. 144 pages, $9.95

WORLD CHAMPION OPENINGS by Eric Schiller - This serious reference work covers the essential opening theory and moves of every major chess opening and variation as played by all the world champions. Reading as much like an encyclopedia of the must-know openings crucial to every chess player's knowledge as a powerful tool showing the insights, concepts and secrets as used by the greatest players of all time, World Champion Openings (WCO) covers an astounding 100 crucial openings in full conceptual detail (with 100 actual games from the champions themselves)! A must-have book for serious chess players. 384 pages, $18.95

STANDARD CHESS OPENINGS by Eric Schiller - The new definitive standard on opening chess play in the 20th century, this comprehensive guide covers every important opening and variation ever played and currently in vogue. More than 3,000 opening strategies are presented! Differing from previous opening books which rely almost exclusively on bare notation, SCO features substantial discussion and analysis on each opening so that you learn and understand the concepts behind them. Includes more than 250 completely annotated games (including a game representative of each major opening) and more than 1,000 diagrams! For modern players at any level, this is the standard reference book necessary for competitive play. A must have for serious chess players!!! 768 pages, $24.95

UNORTHODOX CHESS OPENINGS by Eric Schiller - The exciting guide to every major unorthodox chess opening, contains more than 1,500 weird, contentious, controversial, un-conventional, arrogant, and outright strange opening strategies. From their tricky tactical surprises to their bizarre names, these openings fly in the face of tradition. You'll meet such openings as the Orangutang, Raptor Variation, Halloween Gambit, Double Duck, Franken-stein-Dracula Variation, and even the Drunken King! These openings are a sexy and exotic way to spice up a game and a great weapon to spring on unsuspecting and often unpre-pared opponents. More than 750 diagrams show essential positions. 528 pages, $24.95

GAMBIT OPENING REPERTOIRE FOR WHITE by Eric Schiller - Players who enjoy at-tacking from the very first move are rewarded here with a powerful repertoire of brilliant gambits. Starting with 1.e4 or 1.d4 and using sharp weapons such as the Göring Gambit (Accepted and Declined), Halasz Gambit, Alapin Gambit, Ulysses Gambit, Short Attack and more, to put great pressure on opponents, Schiller presents a complete attacking repertoire to use against the most popular defenses, including the Sicilian, French, Scandinavian, Caro-Kann, Pirc, Alekhine, and other Open Game positions. 192 pages, $14.95.

GAMBIT OPENING REPERTOIRE FOR BLACK by Eric Schiller - For players that like exciting no-holds-barred chess, this versatile gambit repertoire shows Black how to take charge with aggressive attacking defenses against any orthodox White opening move; 1.e4, 1.d4 and 1.c4. Learn the Scandinavian Gambit against 1.e4, Schara Gambit and Queen's Gambit Declined variations against 1.d4, and flank and unorthodox gambits. Black learns the secrets of seizing the initiative from White's hands, usually by investing a pawn or two, to begin powerful attacks that can send White to defeat. 176 pages, $14.95.

COMPLETE DEFENSE TO QUEEN PAWN OPENINGS *by Eric Schiller* - This aggressive counterattacking repertoire covers Black opening systems against virtually every chess opening except for 1.e4 (including most flank games), based on the exciting and powerful Tarrasch Defense, an opening that helped bring championships to Kasparov and Spassky. Black learns to use the Classical Tarrasch, Symmetrical Tarrasch, Asymmetrical Tarrasch, Marshall and Tarrasch Gambits, and Tarrasch without Nc3, to achieve an early equality or even an outright advantage in the first moves. 288 pages, $16.95.

COMPLETE DEFENSE TO KING PAWN OPENINGS *by Eric Schiller* - Learn a complete defensive system against 1.e4. This powerful repertoire not only limits White's ability to obtain any significant opening advantage but allows Black to adopt the flexible Caro-Kann formation, the favorite weapon of many of the greatest chess players. All White's options are explained, and a plan is given for Black to combat them all. Analysis is up-to-date and backed by examples from games of top stars. Detailed index lets you follow openings from the point of a specific player or through its history. 240 pages, $16.95.

HYPERMODERN OPENING REPERTOIRE FOR WHITE *by Eric Schiller* - Instead of placing pawns in the center of the board as traditional openings advise, this complete opening repertoire for White shows you how to stun opponents by "allowing" Black to occupy the center with its pawns, while building a crushing phalanx from the flanks, ready to smash the center apart with Black's slightest mistake. White's approach is simple to learn–because White almost always develops pieces in the same manner–but can be used against all defenses no matter what Black plays! Plentiful diagrams and explanations illustrate every concept, with games from the greatest players showing the principles in action.The Réti and English openings, which form the basis of the Hypermodern, lead to lively games with brilliant sacrifices and subtle maneuvering. 304 pages, $16.95.

SECRETS OF THE SICILIAN DRAGON by *Eduard Gufeld and Eric Schiller* - The mighty Dragon Variation of the Sicilian Defense is one of the most exciting openings in chess. Everything from opening piece formation to the endgame, including clear explanations of all the key strategic and tactical ideas, is covered in full conceptual detail. Instead of memorizing a jungle of variations, you learn the really important ideas behind the opening, and how to adapt them at the chessboard. Special sections on the heroes of the Dragon show how the greatest players handle the opening. The most instructive book on the Dragon written! 208 pages, $14.95.

SECRETS OF THE KING'S INDIAN by *Eduard Gufeld and Eric Schiller*
The King's Indian Defense is the single most popular chess opening and offers great opportunities for spectacular attacks and clever defenses. Readers learn the fundamental concepts, critical ideas, and hidden resources with special attention given to opening traps and typical tactical and strategic mistakes. All of the major variations are covered, including the Classical, Petrosian, Saemisch, Averbakh, Four Pawns, Fianchetto and unconventional lines. Players learn how the strategies and tactics were applied in the most brilliant games of the most famous players, how they can apply these concepts to their own games, and how to keep the material up to date on the Internet. 240 pages, $14.95.

- MIDDLEGAME/TACTICS/WINNING CONCEPTS -

WINNING CHESS TACTICS *by Bill Robertie* - 14 chapters of winning ideas show the complete explanations and thinking behind every tactical concept: pins, single and double forks, double attacks, skewers, discovered and double checks, multiple threats - and other crushing tactics to gain an immediate edge over opponents. Learn the power tools of tactical play to become a better player. Includes guide to chess notation. 128 pages, $9.95.

303 TRICKY CHESS TACTICS   *Fred Wilson and Bruce Alberston* - Both a fascinating challenge and great training tool, this is a fun and entertaining collection of two and three move tactical surprises for the advanced beginner, intermediate, and expert player. Tactics are arranged by difficulty so that a player may measure progress as he advances from simple to the complex positions. The examples, drawn from actual games, illustrate a wide range of chess tactics from old classics right up to the 1990's. 192 pages, $12.95.

10 MOST COMMON CHESS MISTAKES and How to Fix Them *by Larry Evans* - This fascinating collection of 218 errors, oversights, and outright blunders, not only shows the price great players pay for violating basic principles, but how to avoid these mistakes in your own game. You'll be challenged to choose between two moves, the right one, or the one actually played. From neglecting development, king safety, misjudging threats, and premature attacks, to impulsiveness, snatching pawns, and basic inattention, you receive a complete course in where you can go wrong and how to fix it. 256 pages, $14.95.

ENCYCLOPEDIA OF CHESS WISDOM, The Essential Concepts and Strategies of Smart Chess Play *by Eric Schiller* - The most important concepts, strategies, tactics, wisdom, and thinking that every chessplayer must know, plus the gold nuggets of knowledge behind every attack and defense is collected together in one volume. Step-by-step, from opening, middle and endgame strategy, to psychological warfare and tournament tactics, Schiller shows the thinking behind each essential concept, and through examples, diagrams, and discussions, shows its impact on the game. 432 pages, $19.95.

WORLD CHAMPION COMBINATIONS *by Raymond Keene and Eric Schiller* - Learn the insights, concepts, and moves of the greatest combinations ever by the best players of all time. From Morphy to Alekhine, to Fischer to Kasparov, the incredible combinations and brilliant sacrifices of the 13 World Champions are collected here in the most insightful combinations book yet. Packed with fascinating strategems, 50 annotated games, and great practical advice for your own games, this is a great companion guide to *World Champion Openings* and the other titles in the *World Champion* series. 264 pages, $16.95.

WORLD CHAMPION TACTICS *by Leonid Shamkovich and Eric Schiller* - The authors show how the greatest players who ever lived used their entire arsenal of tactical weapons to bring opponents to their knees. Packed with fascinating strategems, 50 fully annotated games, and more than 200 diagrams, players learn not only the thinking and game plan behind the moves of the champions, but the insights that will allow them to use these brilliancies in their own games. Each tactical concept is fully explained with examples and game situations from the champions themselves. 304 pages, $18.95.

WORLD CHAMPION CHESS MATCHES *by Eduard Gufeld and Efim Lazerev* - The exciting highlights and great games of every World Championship chess match are recounted in Gufeld's lively style, with anecdotes, little-known stories and hundreds of key position diagrams. Gufeld does much more than present the in-depth analysis and thinking behind the moves of the greatest of the greats: Gurus, paraphsycologists, dirty tricks, psychological warfare and all the side shows that have brought worldwide media attention to each contest are brought to life. Gufeld should know these secrets; he has played with the very best for decades, and has to his credit the scalps of three former world champions and eight world championship candidates. 304 pages, $18.95.

- MATES & ENDGAMES -

303 TRICKY CHECKMATES *by Fred Wilson and Bruce Alberston* - Both a fascinating challenge and great training tool, this collection of two, three, and bonus four move checkmates is great for advanced beginning, intermediate and expert players. Mates are in order of difficulty, from simple to complex. Learn the standard patterns and stratagems for cornering the king: corridor and support mates, attraction and deflection sacrifices, pins and annihilation, the quiet move, the dreaded *zugzwang*. Examples from actual games, illustrate a wide range of tactics from old classics up to the 90's. 192 pages, $12.95.

365 ESSENTIAL ENDGAME POSITIONS *by Eric Schiller* - From basic mates to sophisticated double-rook endgames, every essential endgame concept is explained. An enormous 365 positions show endgames of every stripe; from king and pawn and bishops vs. knights, rook and pawn vs. two minor pieces, tricky endgames where no pawns are present, and much more.The thinking behind every position is explained in words (unlike diagram-only books) so that you learn which positions are winning, drawn, or cannot be saved. Frequent diagrams show both starting and target positions, so you can visualize the end goals, and steer the middlegame into a successful endgame mate. 400 pages, $18.95.

BASIC ENDGAME STRATEGY: Kings, Pawns and Minor Pieces *by Bill Robertie* - Learn the mating principles and combinations needed to finish off opponents. From the four basic checkmates using the King with the queen, rook, two bishops, and bishop/knight combinations, to King/pawn, King/Knight and King/Bishop endgames, you'll learn the essentials of translating small edges into decisive checkmates. Learn the 50-move rule, and the combinations of pieces that can't force a mate against a lone King. 144 pages, $12.95.

BASIC ENDGAME STRATEGY: Rooks and Queens by Bill Robertie - The companion guide to *Basic Endgame Strategy: Kings, Pawns and Minor Pieces*, you'll learn the mating principles and combinations of the Queen and Rook with King, how to turn middlegame advantages into victories, by creating passed pawns, using the King as a weapon, clearing the way for rook mates, and other endgame combinations. 144 pages, $12.95.

MASTER CHECKMATE STRATEGY *by Bill Robertie* - Learn the basic combinations, plus advanced, surprising and unconventional mates, the most effective pieces needed to win, and how to mate opponents with just a pawn advantage. also, how to work two rooks into an unstoppable attack; how to wield a queen advantage with deadly intent; how to coordinate pieces of differing strengths into indefensible positions of their opponents; when it's best to have a knight, and when a bishop to win. 144 pages, $9.95

- BEGINNING AND GENERAL CHESS BOOKS -

THE BASICS OF WINNING CHESS *by Jacob Cantrell* - A great first book of chess, in one easy reading, beginner's learn the moves, pieces, basic rules and principles of play, standard openings, and both Algebraic and English chess notation. The basic ideas of the winning concepts and strategies of middle and end game play are also shown. Includes example games of champions. 64 pages, $4.95.

BEGINNING CHESS PLAY *by Bill Robertie* - Step-by-step approach uses 113 diagrams to teach the basics of chess: opening, middle and endgame strategies, principles of development, pawn structure, checkmates, openings and defenses, how to write and read chess notation, join a chess club, play in tournaments, use a chess clock, and get rated. Two annotated games illlustrate strategic thinking for easy learning. 144 pages, $9.95

WHIZ KIDS TEACH CHESS Eric Schiller & the Whiz Kids - Today's greatest young stars, some perhaps to be future world champions, present a fascinating look at the world of chess. Each tells of their successes, failures, world travels, and love of chess, show off their best moves, and admit to their most embarrassing blunders. This is more than just a fascinating look at prodigies like Vinay Bhat and Irina Krush, it's also a primer featuring diagrams, explanations, and winning ideas for young players. 144 oversized pages, $14.95.

CARDOZA'S COMPLETE BOOK OF BEGINNING CHESS *by Raymond Keene* - Complete step-by-step course shows how to play and deepen one's understanding of chess while keeping the game fun and exciting. Fascinating chapters on chess heroes and lessons one can learn from these greats, basic chess openings, strategy, tactics, the best games of chess ever played, and the history of chess round out a player's education. Readers also learn how to use chess notation and all the basic concepts of game play – castling, pawn promotion, putting an opponent into check, the five ways of drawing or stalemating games, en passant, actual checkmate, and much more. 400 pages, $19.95.

CHESS PLAYER'S GUIDE TO THE INTERNET *by Eric Schiller* - The internet is the new medium of chess! Every day, hundreds of thousands of enthusiasts from almost 150 countries meet and compete on the internet for games, tournaments, and chat around the clock, or to simply meet new friends. This fun and informational book is the indispensable guide to internet chess: How to play online, earn official rankings, find the best sites and newsgroups, visit chess bookstores, shop for chess items, watch grandmaster and championship games live, seek advice, research openings and strategies, get software, and play in tournaments. Buyers of this book get free membership to chess-playing sites, discounts on chess items, and more than $50 in discounts!!! 128 pages, $12.95.

CARDOZA PUBLISHING ONLINE

For the Latest in Chess Software and Books
by the World's Best Chess Writers

www.cardozapub.com

To find out about our latest chess and backgammon publications, to order books and software from third parties, or simply to keep aware of our latest publications and activities in the chess world:

1. Go online: www.cardozapub.com
2. Use E-Mail: cardozapub@aol.com
3. Call toll free: 800-577-WINS (800-577-9467)
4. Write: Cardoza Publishing, 132 Hastings Street, Brooklyn, NY 11235

Use order form below to order Cardoza Publishing products.

BECOME A BETTER CHESS PLAYER!

YES! I want to be a winner! Rush me the following items: (Write in choices below):

Quantity	Your Book Order	Price	

MAKE CHECKS TO:
Cardoza Publishing
132 Hastings Street
Brooklyn, NY 11235

CHARGE BY PHONE:
Toll-Free: 1-800-577-WINS
Local Phone: 718-743-5229
Fax Orders: 718-743-8284
E-Mail Orders: CardozaPub@aol.com

	Price	
Subtotal		
Postage/Handling: First Item	$5	00
Additional Postage		
Total Amount Due		

SHIPPING CHARGES: For US orders, include $5.00 postage/handling 1st book ordered; for each additional book, add $1.00. For Canada/Mexico, double above amounts, quadruple (4X) for all other countries. Orders outside U.S., money order payable in U.S. dollars on U.S. bank only.

NAME _____

ADDRESS _____

CITY _____ STATE _____ ZIP _____

30 day money back guarantee!   World Champion Tactics